Wedding Wit

First Published in Great Britain 2011 by

Prion Books
An imprint of the
Carlton Publishing Group
20 Mortimer Street
London W1T3JW

A catalogue record for this book is available from the British Library

ISBN 978-1-85375-804-1

Printed in the UK by CPI Mackays, Chatham, ME5 8TD

10 9 8 7 6 5 4 3 2 1

Wedding Wit

Over 1,000 Humorous
Quotes on Tying the Knot

Michael Powell

PRION

Introduction

Few occasions generate as much public curiosity and as many conflicting feelings and column inches as a wedding; those of celebrities and commoners alike are always in the news, because a story is always elevated to a drama when it involves a bride and groom.

However, a wedding has a paradox wired into its DNA – it is both a beginning and an end, theatrical and intimate, public and deeply personal, funny and tragic, as the numerous wedding mishap viral videos on the internet bear out. This is what makes it such a rich seam for humour.

There's the awkward or lacklustre proposal, the excitement-cum-panic-cum-drudgery of the preparations, the diplomatic time-bomb of the invitees, the crippling expenses, the mother of the bride's polyester hat, the best man accidentally pushing the bride into a fountain, jaded guests who would rather be somewhere else, vol-au-vents, chicken legs, cheesecake, vol-au-vents, chicken legs, cheesecake, inarticulate DJs and embarrassing relatives dancing, honeymoon capers and when it's all over the scary prospect of 50 years of wedded bliss.

From the shotgun ceremony to the absurd excesses of celebrity nuptials, a wedding accommodates so many competing interests that it always treads a path between high drama and farce. This is why, time and time again, it continues to serve up the funnies.

Michael Powell, 2011

Contents

Marriage

We've fallen in love with the wedding industry when what we need is a marriage industry.

Bridget Brennan

If mum calls, tell her I'm shitting . . . Son, marriage is about not having to lie about taking a shit.

Justin Halpern

Shit My Dad Says

MARRIAGE, n. The state or condition of a community consisting of a master, a mistress and two slaves, making in all, two.

Ambrose Bierce

The Devil's Dictionary

Marriage is when you get to keep your girl and don't have to give her back to her parents.

Eric

age 6

There's a way of transferring funds that's even faster than electronic banking. It's called marriage.
Ronnie Shakes

Marriage is like a cage; one sees the birds outside desperate to get in, and those inside desperate to get out.
Michel de Montaigne

To marry is to halve your rights and double your duties.
Arthur Schopenhauer

It is most unwise for people in love to marry.
George Bernard Shaw

Marriage is like the Middle East – there's no solution.
Shirley Valentine
Shirley Valentine

Here's to matrimony, the high sea for which no compass has yet been invented!
Heinrich Heine

Marriage is like a bank account.
You put it in, you take it out, you lose interest.
Irwin Corey

If we take matrimony at its lowest, we regard it as a sort of friendship recognised by the police.
Robert Louis Stevenson

The appropriate age for marriage is around
eighteen for girls and thirty-seven for men.
Aristotle

Marriage is a wonderful invention; then again, so is a bicycle repair kit.
Billy Connolly

Marriage – a book of which the first chapter is written in poetry and
the remaining chapters written in prose.
Beverly Nichols

Marriage isn't a process of prolonging the life of love, but of
mummifying the corpse.
P G Wodehouse

My dad says finding somebody that when you're old is going to wipe
your arse – that's marriage.
Jason Manford

Marriage is the death of hope.
Woody Allen

Love is blind – marriage is the eye-opener.
Pauline Thomason

Marriage is bliss. Ignorance is bliss. Therefore . . .
Anon

I'm telling you, married people are the enemy.
Miranda (Cynthia Nixon)
Sex and The City

Marriage is not just spiritual communion, it is also remembering to take out the trash.
Joyce Brothers

Marriage isn't a word . . . it's a sentence.
King Vidor
The Crawl

Marriage is like pi – natural, irrational, and very important.
Lisa Hoffman

Marriage is like putting your hand into a bag of snakes in the hope of pulling out an eel.
Leonardo Da Vinci

Marriage is like twirling a baton, turning hand-springs or eating with chopsticks. It looks easy until you try it.
Helen Rowland

Marriage, like a submarine, is only safe if you get all the way inside.
Frank Pittman

Soul Mates

Gravitation is not responsible for people falling in love.
Albert Einstein

Summer: I woke up one morning and I just knew.
Tom: Knew what?
Summer: What I was never sure of with you.
500 Days of Summer

There I was, standing there in the church, and for the first time in my whole life I realised I totally and utterly loved one person. And it wasn't the person next to me in the veil. It's the person standing opposite me now . . . in the rain.
Charles (Hugh Grant)
Four Weddings and a Funeral

Before I met my husband I'd never fallen in love,
though I've stepped in it a few times.
Rita Rudner

Sometimes if you're lucky, someone comes into your life who'll take up a place in your heart that no one else can fill, someone who's tighter than a twin, more with you than your own shadow, who gets deeper under your skin than your own blood and bones.

Snoop Dogg

Twenty-three is the best age because
you know the person FOREVER by then.

Camille
age 10

I dunno, she's got gaps, I got gaps, together we fill gaps.

Rocky (Sylvester Stallone)
Rocky

God says to Adam, "What would you like in a wife?"
"Hmmm," says Adam, "I'd like her to be the most beautiful creature in the world. I'd like her to do whatever I tell her to. I'd like her to work hard, be smart, enjoy being with me."
"Hmmm", God says, "I can do it, but it'll cost you an arm and a leg."
"Oh," says Adam, "Well, what can I get for a rib?"

Michael Bradley

I always just hoped that... that I'd meet some nice friendly girl, like the look of her, hope the look of me didn't make her physically sick, then pop the question and, um, settle down and be happy. It worked for my parents. Well, apart from the divorce and all that.

Tom (James Fleet)
Four Weddings and a Funeral

We married for better or worse –
he couldn't do better and I couldn't do worse.

Anon

When Charlotte really liked a guy, she said his whole name – it helped
her to imagine their future monogrammed towels.

Carrie Bradshaw (Sarah Jessica Parker)
Sex and The City

Being married to Marge is like being married to my best friend – and he
lets me feel his boobs.

Homer Simpson

It should be a very happy marriage –
they're both so in love with him.

Irene Thomas

I was watching TV and there was a Spice Girls video on and I said, "See
the girl in the dark short dress! I'm going to marry her."

David Beckham

No matter who you marry, you wake up married to someone else.

Marlon Brando

ITN Reporter Anthony Carthew: And, I suppose, in love?
Lady Diana Spencer: Of course.
Prince Charles: Whatever 'in love' means.
ITN news report

A soul mate marriage . . . means . . . they don't ever want to blow out
that little light inside you. And you feel the same way about them.
Diane Sollee

When *Top Gun* came out my sisters were like, "Oh, my God, Top Gun!
Tom Cruise!" And I very confidently said, "I'm going to marry him one
day" . . . It was just . . . Why not? He'll like me. I'm fun.
Katie Holmes

When marrying, ask yourself this question: Do you believe that
you will be able to converse well with this person into your old age?
Everything else in marriage is transitory.
Friedrich Nietzsche

Your soul mate is the person that pushes all your buttons – pisses you
off on a regular basis.
Madonna

I wouldn't be caught dead marrying a woman old enough to be my wife.
Tony Curtis

Miranda: I love how they say, "Until recently, the bride 'worked'".
Carrie: Yeah, meaning she quit her job as soon as she found her soul-
mate-slash-investment-banker.
Sex and The City

He's sophisticated, he brings her flowers and candy, he dines by candlelight. Her last boyfriend thought it was enough to spray her name on a fence.

Tim Conway

A man should be taller, older, heavier, uglier and hoarser than his wife.

Edgar Watson How

When a scholar goes to seek out a bride he should take along an ignoramus as an expert.

The Talmud

I thought I was promiscuous, but it turns out I was just thorough – to get the right one.

Russell Brand

I'm married to the person I'd be jerking off to.

Pete Wentz

Don't marry the person you think you can live with; marry only the individual you think you can't live without.

James C. Dobson

People shop for a bathing suit with more care than they do a husband or wife. The rules are the same. Look for something you'll feel comfortable wearing. Allow for room to grow.

Erma Bombeck

No person really decides before they grow up who they're going to marry. God decides it all way before, and you get to find out later who you're stuck with.

Kirsten

age 10

Love matches, so called, have illusion for their father
and need for their mother.

Friedrich Nietzsche

Marriage is a matter of give and take, but so far I haven't been able to find anybody who'll take what I have to give.

Cass Daley

Before you get married you should meet your fiance's parents. It is not enough that you like his parole officer.

Phyllis Diller

A man likes his wife to be just clever enough to appreciate his cleverness, and just stupid enough to admire it.

Israel Zangwill

Men marry because they are tired, women because they are curious. Both are disappointed.

Oscar Wilde

I married beneath me. All women do.
Nancy Astor

You've got to be married, haven't you?
You can't go through life being happy.
Colin Crompton

I would split the pack and always come up with a Queen of Hearts.
Because I'm into mysticism, it filled my heart and made me stop
worrying about whether I was with the right person.
Robbie Williams

I was gonna do that mail-order bride thing. You don't know, because
if you ain't home and your neighbour signs for her, she's out there
mowing his lawn.
Reno Collier

When an actor marries an actress they both fight for the mirror.
Burt Reynolds

The conception of two people living together for twenty-five years
without having a cross word suggests a lack of spirit only to be admired
in sheep.
A P Herbert

Don't marry a woman with big hands.
It makes your dick look small.
Anon

There is nothing so difficult to marry as a large nose.
Oscar Wilde

You got to find somebody who likes the same stuff. Like, if you like sports, she should like it that you like sports, and she should keep the chips and dip coming.
Alan
age 10

God help the man who won't marry until he finds a perfect woman, and God help him still more if he finds her.
Benjamin Tillet

Perfection is what American women expect to find in their husbands . . . but English women only hope to find in their butlers.
W. Somerset Maugham

It's true that I did get the girl, but then my grandfather always said, "Even a blind chicken finds a few grains of corn now and then".
Lyle Lovett
on marrying Julia Roberts

I think men who have a pierced ear are better prepared for marriage. They've experienced pain and bought jewellery.
Rita Rudner

I remember one of the first things I said to him was, "Tell me everything that you think I'm not going to like about you". And he went on for about an hour and a half. Then I still married him.

Kate Hudson
on ex-husband Chris Robinson

Strong women only marry weak men.
Bette Davis

When a man opens a car door for his wife,
it's either a new car or a new wife.
Prince Philip

Of course, I do have a slight advantage over the rest of you. It helps in a pinch to be able to remind your bride that you gave up a throne for her.
Edward VIII

—Name something a girl should know about a man before marrying him.
—His name.
Family Fortunes

Men are like a deck of cards. You need a heart to love him, a diamond to marry him, a club to bash his head in with . . . and a spade to bury him with.
Anon

I married the first man I ever kissed. When I tell this to my children they just about throw up.
Barbara Bush

Strike an average between what a woman thinks of her husband a month before she marries him and what she thinks of him a year afterward, and you will have the truth about him.

H.L. Mencken

When Mel told his Jewish mother he was marrying an Italian girl, she said: "Bring her over. I'll be in the kitchen – with my head in the oven".

Anne Bancroft

(married Mel Brooks)

You send away to the Philippines, and they send you a wife. The only thing is, once you're on their mailing list, they keep sending you a relative a month whether you want it or not.

Adam Ferrara

Every mother generally hopes that her daughter will snag a better husband than she managed to do but she's certain that her boy will never get as great a wife as his father did.

Anon

In many ways we feel like we already are married. I know I'm with the woman I want to spend the rest of my life with. So the wedding – that's just the party.

Tom Cruise

Marry not a golfer, footballer or tennis player.
For love means nothing to them.

Michael Bradley

My wife picked me out of a soccer sticker book,
and I chose her off the telly . . . It felt straight away like we'd always
been meant to be together.
David Beckham

I've been brought up to believe that you marry the first man that you
meet. If that was the case I would have married my Uncle Shazad – but
at 13 I think I was too old for him.
Shazia Mirza

No matter how old you are, it's always going to be your first marriage
and no life experience is going to make you a better judge of who you
should marry.
Hikaru Utada

Don't marry someone you would not be friends with if there was no sex
between you.
William Glasser

It ought to be illegal for an artist to marry. If the artist must marry let
him find someone more interested in art, or his art, or the artist part of
him, than in him.
Ezra Pound

I was very lucky I married 'the one'.
On a scale of one to ten, he was the one.
Mary Bourke

My parents really want me to get married, but Asian men don't really want to marry me. Because I speak.
Shazia Mirza

Marry an outdoors woman. Then if you throw her out into the yard for the night, she can still survive.
W. C. Fields

Adam knew Eve his wife and she conceived.
It is a pity that this is still the only knowledge of their wives at which some men seem to arrive.
Francis H. Bradley

They have come up with a perfect understanding. He won't try to run her life, and he won't try to run his, either.
Anon

The first time you marry for love, the second for money, and the third for companionship.
Jackie Kennedy

Most girls seem to marry men who happen to be like their fathers. Maybe that's why so many mothers cry at weddings.
Jenny Éclair

Marriage is an alliance entered into by a man who can't sleep with the window shut, and a woman who can't sleep with the window open.
George Bernard Shaw

I'm performing naked cartwheels. I'm very excited.

Brad Pitt

on marrying Jennifer Aniston

When I talk about my husband, I feel as if people roll their eyes . . .
They can't grasp that I'm old enough to be married.

Megan Fox

on Brian Austin Green

People say you just know, and we just knew . . . she was pregnant.

Hal Cruttenden

Other Reasons to Tie the Knot

I was so excited about my wedding because
I couldn't wait to meet my husband.
Shazia Mirza

Just settle. They're settling for you; you settle for them.
Find someone you can sleep next to without throwing up,
and marry them.
Tom Papa

I like being married for two reasons. One, I got really tired of dating,
and two, I got really tired of exercising.
Jeff Stilson

I always wanted a beautiful loving wife
and she always wanted to be a citizen.
Emo Philips

I'm going to marry a Jewish woman because I like the idea of getting up
Sunday morning and going to the deli.
Michael J. Fox

If both people make $300,000, they'll pay more than $18,000 in taxes by filing jointly. That's about the cost of the wedding.

John Battaglia

No woman marries for money; they are all clever enough, before marrying a millionaire, to fall in love with him first.

Cesare Pavese

If marriage didn't exist, would you invent it?
Would you go, "Baby, this shit we got together, it's so good we gotta get the government in on this shit"?

Doug Stanhope

It's important to think out marriage in general because it's a huge commitment. Besides that, I hate to say it, but it's a lot of paperwork and a lot of emotions.

Carmen Electra

Most men, you see, marry for safety;
they choose a woman who will make them feel like a man but never really challenge them to be one.

John Eldredge

Men who marry for gratification, propagation or the matter of buttons or socks must expect to cope with – and deal in – a certain amount of quibble, subterfuge, concealment, and double, deep-dyed prevarication.

Elbert Hubbard

If I could meet a girl with puppy breath, I'd marry her. Twelve tits wouldn't be bad, either.
Todd Glass

A bachelor's life is no life for a single man.
Samuel Goldwyn

My first marriage was not happy. I married him because I was impressed that he knew which wines to order and how to leave his visiting card.
Jean Seberg

Many a man in love with a dimple makes the mistake of marrying the whole girl.
Stephen Leacock

Sometimes I worry that I don't wanna get married as much as I want to get dipped in a vat of warm, rising bread dough. That might feel pretty good, too.
Maria Bamford

Marriage is our last, best chance to grow up.
Joseph Barth

I have a high state of resentment for the conformity in this country. If you're not married and having children, it's like your life is empty or you're a communist meanie.
Bill Maher

Eighty-four, because at that age, you don't have to work any more, and you can spend all your time loving each other in your bedroom.

Carolyn
age 8, on the proper age to get married

I think we were filling in some forms for wills or insurance, and I just thought, let's just make this as legal as we can. It was with a bunch of Russian mail-order brides, literally.

Cheyenne Jackson
(married Monte Lapka)

A man who marries a woman to educate her falls a victim to the same fallacy as the woman who marries a man to reform him.

Elbert Hubbard

I always remember the old song, "Wedding bells are breaking up that old gang of mine" . . . You're going to grow up. You're going to get married. You're going to get girlfriends and have babies and things, and you don't do that in a band.

Paul McCartney

If you are so obsessed with Bridget Jones, why don't you just marry her? . . . 'Cos then she'd definitely shag me.

Daniel Cleaver (Hugh Grant)
Bridget Jones: The Edge of Reason

If you made a list of the reasons why any couple got married, and another list of the reasons for their divorce, you'd have a hell of a lot of overlapping.

Mignon McLaughlin

When you're bored with yourself,
marry and be bored with someone else.
King Edward VIII

I remember when I was in school, they would ask, "What are you going to be when you grow up?" and then you'd have to draw a picture of it. I drew a picture of myself as a bride.
Gwen Stefani

One has to be able to count, if only so that at 50 one doesn't marry a girl of 20.
Maxim Gorky

Jeremy: Are you getting married or not?
Mark: I don't know. I don't want to end up on my own like Miss Havisham, wanking into a flannel, but I do feel very strongly that it's not . . . right.
Peep Show

I think some people are desperate to get married because they want a big white wedding, whereas I get to be the centre of attention every day, so it's not quite so pressing.
Lucy Porter

At last I've got someone to take the rubbish out. And now I don't have to worry if the car goes wrong or a lightbulb needs changing. That's all marriage is, isn't it?
Meera Syal

I had to marry a challenge because otherwise I would just get bored.
Whatever else Guy is, he's never boring.
Madonna

I just felt like I needed to dive in.
Robin Wright Penn
(married Sean Penn)

Do you think Prince Charles went for Camilla Parker-Bowles because
that's what Diana would have looked like if she survived the crash?
Frankie Boyle

I consider myself to be smart and a good mother but it's taken
me this long to realise you don't have to marry a guy after
three days or dump him.
Sheena Easton

No man should marry until he has studied anatomy and dissected at
least one woman.
Honoré de Balzac

If I get married, I want to be very married.
Audrey Hepburn

Now, it's true I married my wife for her looks . . . but not the ones she's
been giving me lately.
Jeff Foxworthy

Life's never dull with him – that's why I married him . . .
That's why I'm marrying him!
Katy Perry
The Graham Norton Show

Marry Prince William? I'd love that.
Who wouldn't want to be a princess?
Britney Spears

I'm officially out of men to f**k. I have to get married or move.
Samantha Jones (Kim Cattrall)
Sex and The City

Having a baby. That pretty much decided it. So we don't have a little
bastard running around.
Milla Jovovich

The trouble with many married people is that they are trying to get
more out of marriage than there is in it.
Elbert Hubbard

My grandmother doesn't want me to marry a non-Jew. She's always
saying things like, "You don't want your kids growing up wearing a
cross, do you?" And I'm like, "I do if they're fighting vampires". Let's
not rule anything out for little Buffy Kaplan.
Myq Kaplan

Dammit sir, it's your duty to get married.
You can't be always living for pleasure.
Oscar Wilde

Do not choose your wife at a dance,
but in the field among the harvesters.
Czech Proverb

I want a man who's kind and understanding. Is that too much to ask of
a millionaire?
Zsa Zsa Gabor

One of the best things about marriage is that it gets young people to
bed at a decent hour.
M M Musselman

The way taxes are, you might as well marry for love.
Joe E Lewis

Duncan: I like stability, I like routine. I like knowing there's people
waiting for me at home. I guess that makes me sound pretty dull.
Miranda: Are you kidding? You're the heterosexual holy grail.
Sex and The City

I didn't marry the cutthroat, ruthless, gimme-all-your-money lawyer. No, I married the pay-me-what-you-can-whenever-you-can-I-just-want-to-see-justice-served lawyer . . . I got so ripped off . . . it's like I'm having sex with a rock star, but he's with a Christian band.

Cory Kahaney

When you see what some women marry, you realize how they must hate to work for a living.

Helen Rowland

The dread of loneliness is greater than the fear of bondage, so we get married.

Cyril Connolly

If a man works like a horse for his money, there are a lot of girls anxious to take him down the bridal path.

Marty Allen

I get to ask him to feed the dogs more often!

Hilary Duff

when asked if getting married had changed anything

What a valiant woman! It is a pity that Elizabeth and I cannot marry. Our children would have ruled the world.

Pope Sixtus V

on Queen Elizabeth I of England

Edina: Who bloody needs 'em? Upper classes, who bloody needs 'em, sweetheart? They're all inbred anyway, aren't they?

Patsy: Yeah, just a talking neck! Most of them have done away with features altogether! They have to marry a bit of common every now and again to ensure bone development!

Absolutely Fabulous

If you marry the wrong person for the wrong reasons, then no matter how hard you work, it's never going to work, because then you have to completely change yourself, completely change them, completely – by that time, you're both dead.

Anne Bancroft

Proposal and Engagement

Ray: Please marry me, Bev. Because I'm shit without you.
Beverly: Oh how romantic . . . a marriage proposal that contains the
word "shit".
Riding in Cars with Boys

Emily, I have a confession to make. I really am a horse doctor. But
marry me, and I'll never look at another horse.
Dr. Hackenbush (Groucho Marx)
A Day at the Races

I've never had a diamond before, and now I've got a diamond
surrounded by other diamonds and diamonds in places where, frankly,
you don't need diamonds at all, and I would have been happy with a
piece of twine. So, yes, of course I said yes.
Summer Phoenix
(married Casey Affleck)

He proposed on Valentine's Day, although he didn't do it face to face,
he did it in one of the little Valentine bits in the paper. I think he had
to pay for it by the word because it just said "LEE LOVE DAWN
MARRIAGE?" which, you know, I like, because it's not often you get
something that's both romantic and thrifty.

Dawn (Lucy Davis)
The Office

It is always incomprehensible to a man that a woman should ever refuse
an offer of marriage.

Jane Austen

It took great courage to ask a beautiful young woman
to marry me. Believe me, it is easier to play the whole of Petrushka on
the piano.

Arthur Rubinstein

I came home to find he had drawn a huge circle on the wall and inside
had written in 2ft-high letters: 'Marry me'. I wrote underneath: 'Yes'.

Judy Cook
on Peter Cook

I knew we were going to marry some day, but I was absolutely surprised
when he actually proposed. And surprised he had bought a ring. I ran
around the yard screaming.

Jennifer Garner

I went to the terrace, still in a foul mood, and suddenly noticed
he was kneeling. I had seen some ants earlier and thought he was
looking for them.

Amanda Redman

Engagement rings are pointless. Indians gave cows . . .
Oh, sorry, congrats on proposing. We good now? Can I finish my
Indian story?

Justin Halpern
Shit My Dad Says

[Seal] took me by helicopter. He had an igloo built there, and they'd
brought up everything: a bed with sheets inside the igloo, rose
petals everywhere, candles. Very, very romantic! There was food and
champagne, and then the helicopter left.

Heidi Klum

I literally stalked her for weeks until she said yes. They say it's not
stalking if she says yes.

Josh Duhamel
on Fergie

If I'd known so many people would ask me how I proposed, I would
have done it in some more theatrical way.

Jeff Richmond
(married Tina Fey)

We are no closer to getting married than we were years ago. It's like a car stalled at the side of the road.

Holly Madison

on Hugh Hefner

How much better would it be if it was an actual equal exchange . . . like whatever ring she picked out she had to buy you something for equal or greater value? "Oh, you want the one-carat princess cut? That's cool, then buy me a solid gold cowboy hat."

Alfonso Ochoa

I'd actually stopped drinking by then, so I should have been sober enough to know what I was doing, but I didn't. So after she accepted, I got drunk . . . I knew it was over before it had begun.

Richard Burton

on his second marriage to Elizabeth Taylor

My most brilliant achievement was my ability to be able to persuade my wife to marry me.

Winston Churchill

Every night we looked into each other's eyes and I was thinking, "Please ask me, please ask me". Then, when we finally talked about the idea of getting married, he admitted he was thinking the same. All the time we'd been sending each other subliminal messages.

Katy Perry

An engaged woman is always more agreeable than a disengaged. She is
satisfied with herself. Her cares are over, and she feels that she may exert
all her powers of pleasing without suspicion.

Jane Austen

I'm deluged with marriage proposals. I even get naked photos. Some
women see me in the same way mountaineers see Everest – I'm a big
challenge, but they still want to mount me and stick a flag at the top.

Alan Carr

Will you marry me? Ayda Field, I love you so much. Do you mind
being my betrothed for the end of time?

Robbie Williams

proposing during an Australian radio interview

I'm definitely asking her to marry me and I'm convinced she's
going to say yes. I might pop the question on TV... I'm convinced
Katie's going to feel the same way.

Alex Reid

on Katie Price, who broke up with him after hearing he was going to propose

I've had it for four years, but fortunately it didn't come with an
expiration date.

Shakira

on her engagement ring from lawyer boyfriend Antonio de la Rua

Gloria Cleary: Jeremy, I am so ready to take it to the next level.
Jeremy Grey: Really?
Gloria Cleary: Yeah. Do you want to watch me with another girl? How about those Brazilian twins we met at the ball game?
Jeremy Grey: I was thinking more along the lines of an engagement.

The Wedding Crashers

Clocks stopped, ravens were spotted leaving the Tower and there was a nip in the air down in Hell when Simon Cowell announced on Saturday night that he had met 'the one'. The entertainment supremo's heavily Botoxed face expressed something near emotion as he spoke of his new love, Mezhgan Hussainy.

Bryony Gordon

Tom Cruise and Katie Holmes announced that they have gotten engaged. Afterward, Katie Holmes was very excited and said, "I couldn't believe it when my publicist told me."

Conan O'Brien

India is buzzing over the recent engagement of Bollywood's hottest couple, Aishwarya Rai and Abhishek Bachchan. Or as they're known in the Bollywood tabloids, 'Aishwarishick'.

Amy Poehler

I was mostly touched by how nervous he was. I was like, "You know I'm going to say yes. Why are you so nervous?" But I guess every man gets nervous at that point.

Eva Longoria
on Tony Parker

When David [Arquette] and I got engaged we started therapy together.
I'd heard that the first year of marriage is the hardest, so we decided to
work through all that stuff early.

Courtney Cox

You tell your guy friends you got engaged, it's like hearing someone died.
"What happened, man? Wow. He was so young, man. What happened?
He had his whole life ahead of him. Wow, I just saw him yesterday."

Jim Breuer

He proposed after we saw this very large, cheap ring which people have
been really rude about but I think it's great.

Helen Lederer

finds true love at the age of 44

A woman might as well propose; her husband will claim she did.

Edgar Watson Howe

You're the only boy who ever made me cry, and I decided that if you
could make me cry, I must really love you.

Gracie Allen

accepting a proposal of marriage from George Burns

Will you marry me? Did he leave you any money?
Answer the second question first.

Groucho Marx

I'm afraid I'm very much the traditionalist. I went down on one knee
and dictated a proposal, which my secretary faxed over straight away.

Stephen Fry

I asked my girlfriend, "Will you marry me?"
She said, "We'll have to ask my father". So we had a séance,
and Jack Ruby says, "Hello!"
Emo Philips

Harrison Ford proposed to Calista Flockhart and then slipped the ring
around her waist.
David Letterman

Marry me and you'll be farting through silk
for the rest of your life.
Robert Mitchum

This afternoon he asked me to be his wife,
and I turned him down like a bedspread.
P G Wodehouse

I remember being asked to be married and being really, sort of,
relieved; OK, at least I got asked.
Oprah Winfrey

Miranda: What? Are you f**king kidding me?
Steve: Is that your answer?
Sex and The City

Taming the Beast

I walked down the aisle as Conan the Barbarian and walked back up
again as Arnold the Meek.
Arnold Schwarzenegger

Married men live longer. Yes. And an indoor cat also lives longer.
It's a furball with a broken spirit that can only look out on a
world it can never enjoy.
Bill Maher

I used to love to hunt and shoot stuff and kill stuff, and then I got
married, and now I'm more in touch with my feminine side. I still kill
stuff; I just wear pumps.
Reno Collier

Husbands are like fires. They go out if left unattended.
Zsa Zsa Gabor

A husband is what is left of the lover after the nerve is extracted.
Helen Rowland

He used to basically be a professional prostitute – now he's not.

Katy Perry
on taming Russell Brand

It has been said that a bride's attitude towards her betrothed can be summed up in three words: Aisle, Altar, Hymn.

Frank Muir

Women love scallywags, but some marry them and then try to make them wear a blazer.

David Bailey

Jerry was quite the bachelor when we met. There was nowhere to put your cocktail down in his place. Just the ping-pong table.

Rebecca Romijn
on Jerry O'Connell

The Japanese have a word for it.
It's judo – the art of conquering by yielding.
The Western equivalent of judo is, "Yes, dear".

J P McEnny

You don't marry one person; you marry three: the person you think they are, the person they are, and the person they are going to become as the result of being married to you.

Richard Needham

Why does a woman work ten years to change a man's habits and then complain that he's not the man she married?

Barbra Streisand

I should like to see any kind of a man, distinguishable from a gorilla, that some good and even pretty woman could not shape a husband out of.

Oliver Wendell Holmes, Sr.

I can no longer seduce because I love my husband . . . I don't want to hurt him. I am no longer a man-eater.

Carla Bruni-Sarkozy

Bridegroom: A man who is amazed at the outcome of what he thought was a harmless little flirtation.

Anon

Guests and Invitations

Meet you in Delhi in October. Dates to follow.
Please allow seven days for this event.

Invitation from
Russell Brand and Katy Perry

Wedding invitations, how much are you spending on these? . . . made of
sloth fur or something . . . there's 25 people getting wasted right there,
that's what that could have been.

Rick Mitchell

At my Cornish wedding, a lot of ex-girlfriends turned up.
Then again, family's family.

Paul Kerensa

I'm sorry I won't be able to make it to your imaginary wedding,
but I'm really busy that day. I already have a unicorn baptism and a
leprechaun Bar Mitzvah.

Phoebe (Lisa Kudrow)
Friends

Invite them. A wedding is a loaded gun.
Don't be the asshole staring down the barrel asking which button
makes the boom noise.

Justin Halpern
Shit My Dad Says

Another wedding invitation. And a list. Lovely.

Charles (Hugh Grant)
Four Weddings and a Funeral

A wedding invitation is sent by people who have been saying, "Do we
have to ask them?" to people whose first response is, "How much do
you think we have to spend on them?"

Judith Martin

This wedding is something that I will always, always cherish. It was a
show of love and support and kindness like I'd never seen from the
people, and that's who I entertain. I entertain the people.

Liza Minnelli

A fight broke out at a wedding, and someone went and got a log.

Greg Warren
on one-star weddings

You don't want two presidents at one wedding! All the secret service, guests going through [metal detectors], all the gifts being torn apart.

President Barack Obama
on not being invited to Chelsea Clinton's wedding

Weddings are never about the bride and groom; weddings are public platforms for dysfunctional families.

Lisa Kleypas
Blue-Eyed Devil

I didn't have a big fat Greek wedding,
but I have a lot of fat Greek friends.

Pete Sampras

I hate weddings. When I go to weddings, they all say, "You'll be next!" What I do now is, when I go to funerals, I say to the relatives, "You'll be next!" That shuts them up.

Paul O'Grady

I'm 36, I'm not married – I give up.
I was just at my cousin's wedding. I caught the bouquet. I just took it home and repotted it.

Cathy Ladman

I never go to weddings. Waste of time.
Person can get married a dozen times. Lots of folks do . . .
But a funeral, that's different. You only die once.

Edna Ferber
Giant

I hate weddings . . . They make me feel so unmarried. Actually, even brushing my teeth makes me feel unmarried.

Melissa Bank

The Girls' Guide to Hunting and Fishing

It's amazing what clarity you get from psychotic jealousy.

Julianne Potter (Julia Roberts)

My Best Friend's Wedding

Ben and J-Lo have announced that they want a small wedding. Yeah. So they decided to invite all the people who saw Gigli.

Conan O'Brien

An invitation to a wedding invokes more trouble than a summons to a police court.

William Feather

Prince Charles married Camilla Parker-Bowles. And – get this – Phil Collins was one of the guests at the royal wedding. In fact, at one point Phil Collins looked around and said, "Wow, I'm the best-looking person here."

Conan O'Brien

Just because I have rice on my clothes doesn't mean I've been to a wedding. A Chinese man threw up on me.

Phyllis Diller

I actually performed at an orthodox Jewish wedding, where the men were separated from the women, but they both came together to not enjoy what I was talking about.

Andy Kindler

Making Plans

We're trying to work out a date between the World Cup and the end of
the Formula 1 season.
Bryan McFadden
makes his priorities clear

I know what colour I want my dresses to be,
and bridesmaids' dresses. He wants a cheesecake.
And that's about as far as we've gotten.
DeAnna Pappas

Plan to get married on Friday the 13th. In years to come this will make
it much easier to explain why things turned out badly.
Phyllis Diller

I want the big drama. I always said I don't want a wedding,
I want a parade.
Star Jones

A bridegroom is a man who is never important at a wedding unless he
fails to show up.
Anon

Stacey: You are coming to this wedding fair, aren't you?
Bryn: I can't wait. I was so excited last night, I couldn't get to sleep till half-past ten!
Gavin and Stacey

The guy who said the groom shouldn't see the dress before the big day – I want to shake his hand for getting us out of that particular shopping expedition.
Ed Byrne

Money can't buy you happiness, so you might as well give your money to us
Dave Barry
on the wedding industry

I told a friend I was getting married, and he said, "Have you picked a date yet?" I said, "Wow, you can bring a date to your own wedding? What a country!"
Yakov Smirnoff

There are so many details. It's like an entire industry. You start to feel like, 25 years from now, the only thing anyone will remember is, did you have monogrammed napkins?
John Henson

June is the traditional month for weddings. The other eleven are for divorce.
Joe Hickman

Always get married early in the morning. That way, if it doesn't work out, you haven't wasted a whole day.
Mickey Rooney

Everyone can relate to the frustrations that a wedding involves, such as arguing about stuff you don't really care about.
Ed Byrne

We wanted to get married, but I didn't want to put on a big frock and pay for everyone to have a chicken dinner. I didn't want a register office wedding either. Those are like "Oh, we're married now apparently. What's on the telly?"
Jo Caulfield

A friend of mine is 30 years old, and she's marrying a guy who's 19. I think it could work, yeah – and if they're smart, they'll plan the wedding around the same time as the prom and rent the one tux.
Clinton Jackson

The sum and substance of female education in America, as in England, is training women to consider marriage as the sole object in life, and to pretend that they do not think so.
Harriet Martineau

The average British wedding emits more CO_2 than ten return flights to Thailand.
BBC Bloom

First-time marriers usually prefer to have a traditional wedding,
defined by experts as "a wedding where the flowers alone cost more
than Versailles".
Dave Barry

I'd like to thank Elsie for the flowers.
It was her funeral I nicked them from.
Hugh Dennis
"Bad Things to Say at a Wedding", *Mock The Week*

Don't sweat the small stuff.
In the end, the colour of the flowers doesn't matter.
Beth Ostrosky

Never get married in the morning, because you never know who you'll
meet that night.
Paul Hornung

If you want people to come to your wedding,
don't pick a Tuesday.
Sue Blackhath

Planning the wedding is a trial run for your future marriage.
Tina B. Tessina

Most men haven't been envisioning their wedding day
since they were little.
Kathleen Murray

Am I the only creature with a vagina who thinks that weddings are ridiculous? I'm going to elope. Just me, my hubby, and a minister on a beach in Jamaica.
Megan McCafferty

Weddings are for women, I tell you.
Eric Braeden

I said if you're having a white horse,
I'm putting down ice and skating.
Michael Bublé
on Luisana Loreley Lopilato de la Torre

We're having a little disagreement. What I want is a big church wedding with bridesmaids and flowers and a no-expense-spared reception, and what he wants is to break off our engagement.
Sally Poplin

I don't care what colour napkins are on the table. I don't care. We're just both really laid back. Family, food and fun, that's all we really need. And, oh, yeah, get married.
Carrie Underwood

Emma: Your wedding's gonna be huge, just like your ass at prom.
Liv: Your wedding can suck it.
Bride Wars

Tom Cruise is famously controlling, and he's certainly been in charge of this wedding. Not only did he help choose Katie's wedding dress, but he's been on top of every detail from the menu to the gift bags.

Nina Callaway

The best thing is that since I've been married
I haven't had to plan a wedding.

Ed Byrne

I have never left a wedding saying, "The serviettes were very disappointing, weren't they?" You can spend your life fretting about these things that no-one else notices.

Dave Gorman

I let the wedding get bigger than Big.

Carrie Bradshaw (Sarah Jessica Parker)
Sex and The City

Denise: Did you get that wedding car sorted?
Dave: I've not had time to wipe me arse.
Denise: I know, I've seen your undies.

The Royle Family

I couldn't trust him to turn up on time.
He's terrible at timekeeping.

Piers Morgan
explains why he didn't choose Simon Cowell to be his best man

All I did at my own wedding was show up, as if I were a gate-crasher instead of the bride.
Tatum O'Neal

Pressure? Get married when you want. Your wedding's just one more day in my life I can't wear sweat pants.
Justin Halpern
Shit My Dad Says

We hadn't been planning to do it but we thought it was rather a good idea, so we just did it.
Kate Winslet
on her spur-of-the-moment wedding to Sam Mendes

We like the evenings – I just don't see the point in getting up early to get married.
Dita von Teese
(married Marilyn Manson)

Chelsea Clinton is getting married. Bill and Hillary are thrilled; they say they don't care who the groom is as long as it's not Levi Johnston.
Jay Leno

Never get married in college; it's hard to get a start if a prospective employer finds you've already made one mistake.
Elbert Hubbard

Choosing to be driven to your wedding in a [Armstrong Siddeley] Sapphire is as tasteful and original as choosing 'My Way' to be played at the crematorium as the coffin slides away.

Neil Lyndon

This whole part in between – the planning, the rehearsal dinner, showers and girly stuff – that's the part that's annoying. I just want to roll down the aisle and then I'll be happy.

Pregnant bride-to-be
Bethenny Frankel

In my wedding, they . . . well, in my wife's wedding that I was allowed to go to . . .

Craig Ferguson

By the end of the day we will have a wedding . . . or we will have a hanging. Either way we will have a lot of fun.

Prince John (Richard Lewis)
Robin Hood: Men in Tights

If you're going to do something like getting married, it should have a sense of celebration to it. It should be grand – it doesn't have to be in tracksuits.

Marilyn Manson

If I were your wedding, I'd be sleeping with one eye open.

Liv Lerner (Kate Hudson)
Bride Wars

They're getting married on a yacht. I think this is a good idea. Not only will Pam be the bride, she'll also serve as a flotation device.

David Letterman
on Pamela Anderson's wedding to Kid Rock

I'd seen weddings at City Hall in New York on TV and it was great. You turn up with a money order for $30 the day before to get a licence and then the wedding is so stress free. I was still deciding where to put my handbag and it was all over.

Jo Caulfield

My wife and I were married in a toilet;
it was a marriage of convenience.

Tommy Cooper

It's like Catholics getting married at a Star Trek convention.

Lee Mack
on Tom Cruise choosing to get married in Rome

Eighteen thousand quid, that's how much the average wedding costs . . . My advice: marry a Buddhist. They always want to get married under a tree: "No problem, love. Oak or larch? It's your big day".

Jeff Green

When we arrived we thought, "What an amazing place." So we went to the little Dutch 16th-century church and asked the vicar if we could get married. "Next Tuesday all right?" he said.

Bill Bailey

who got married on the volcanic island of Banda, Indonesia

My advice to anyone is to not get married in Vegas.
Do not get married at the drive-thru in Vegas, especially.
Take your time – enjoy it.

Carmen Electra

Going on a Diet

It's the wedding season again. You can tell because the average bridal magazine currently weighs more than the average bride.

Dave Barry

I wanted junk food – because I've been so good. I said to my sister Haylie, "After the wedding is over, I'm going to eat 16,000 calories!"

Hilary Duff
on her post-wedding diet

I am so paranoid now after what they did to Jennifer Love Hewitt! I'm like, "Oh, my god, if they think she looks bad then I'm screwed".

Katherine Heigl
on dieting

My wedding dress . . . Angel Sanchez designed it, and every time I'd try it on, he'd say, "Sandra, please [lose] five pounds!" I apologize, Angel. I didn't give him those five pounds, but guess what? That round, shiny, happy person was me.

Sandra Bullock

I used to do a bit of material in which I asked what I should do with my used wedding dress. And on one occasion, a bloke shouted out what I thought was "Dye it!" So I said:
"What, you mean lots of different colours?" And he shouted back:
"No! D-I-E-T. Diet!"

Sarah Millican

Inside me there's a thin bride struggling to get out – I can usually sedate her with a bar of chocolate.

Allison Vale

I've got a wedding I've got to go to next week, and I was trying to lose six pounds by the weekend. I don't think I'm going to do it, so I'm going to get my back waxed, and then I'll only have to lose two.

Boris Hamilton

For my wedding I'm trying to trying to get into shape.
The shape I picked is a triangle.

Dawn French

Stag and Hen Night

It's basically macho, competitive bullshit. Just full of undersexed,
pathetic men running around trying to get more pissed.

Alex Collier

Jeremy: Here, Mark, I tell you what.
You piss in this bottle, I'll drink it.
Mark: What . . . what the hell for?
Jeremy: For a laugh, it's a stag.
Mark: No, Jez, if you drank my piss I'd feel violated.

Peep Show

My middle sister organised my hen do in November 2008 (I got married
on New Year's Eve) and I spent 12 hours drinking cava. I got some great
presents, like this 1913 book on marriage which gives you tips about
how not to annoy your husband. I should probably look at it a bit more.

Laura Solon

I'm gonna get Lady Gaga and Taylor Swift to perform a lesbian show
on my lap. I'm gonna shrink them down till they're the size of dollies.

Russell Brand

Hen nights should be banned. You're honour-bound to behave atrociously, then feel terribly ashamed afterwards.

Marian Keyes

Jeremy: Did you slink off to bed before we did the melon-off?
Mark: I believe so. What exactly is –
Jeremy: Two guys get hard-ons, they put melons on their dicks, first melon to fall off loses.
Mark: Right, and who won – Gore Vidal or Dr Jonathan Miller?

Peep Show

The whole wild drinking, chaining somebody to a lamp post is funny, but if anybody did that to me they wouldn't be coming to my wedding.

Robert Kazinsky

We married in a register office opposite Leicester Cathedral. I had been 18 for a week. My young husband had a black eye; there had been a stag night fracas in a chip shop.

Sue Townshend
on her first marriage

20th wedding anniversary this summer.
We've decided to renew my stag do.

Armando Iannucci
Twitter

I've booked us a canal boat near an Iron Age area and you can go and look at the Iron Age or whatever it is you do, I'll make us some steaks and I've sent off for a chess set and I'll learn how to play but if I'm not good enough then there's a computer setting . . .

Jeremy (Robert Webb)
Peep Show

Peter: Do you admit the Brazilian prostitutes were a mistake?
Mark: I do.
Peter: And it would have been much better
if they'd not turned out to be men?
Mark: That is true.

Love, Actually

Jeremy, there are many things I would do to help you but digging a hole in the wintery earth with my bare hands so that you can bury the corpse of a dog you've killed is not one of them.

Mark Corrigan (David Mitchell)
Peep Show

I don't know if you accept them . . . but it's Borders . . . so you can get CDs too, or . . . I don't know if you can get coffees with it.

Tim Key
offers a lap-dancer a £10 book token, *All Bar Luke*

The most sober stag party in the history of nightclubs.

Peter Stringfellow
on Russell Brand's final night of freedom

Last-Minute Jitters

The day of the wedding I got cold feet. Jim had to do a logical cost-benefit analysis of why getting married would be good. We came out in the black.

Gale Anne Hurd
(married James Cameron)

I did have one wobble on the morning of the wedding when I decided I had to go down and cut all the foliage at the front door as I was convinced I wouldn't be able to get out and down the path in my wedding dress.

Lorraine Kelly

You think the night before a Mormon wedding a guy says, "How am I gonna sleep with the same eight women for the rest of my life?"

Eric (Kevin Connolly)
Entourage

Why do you think a bride cries on her wedding day? It's for the love
that this marriage is putting an end to for all eternity.
Nadeem Aslam
Maps for Lost Lovers

On the morning of the wedding, she was in a complete panic. She
said, "Something old, something new – I've got nothing borrowed and
blue!" I said, "You've got a mortgage and varicose veins, will that do?"
Victoria Wood

I know I am a complete disaster, so I am writing this to warn any brides
out there to please take this advice: Do NOT – repeat NOT – leave
everything until the last minute.
Maura Derrane

I'm not marrying out of spite, I'm marrying out of fear.
There's a very big difference.
Mark (David Mitchell)
Peep Show

I think that moment of doubt and faintness comes from all those
imagined and now impossible futures all pressing in on you at once. It
is your last chance to experience them, you see, and they all want to be
lived at that moment.
Sharon Shinn

Oh, you mean, all guys are nervous and anxious [the night before their wedding] . . . and kinda hopes she eats a can of botulism . . . or, or maybe she can hang out with a deer and a hunter accidentally shoots her.

Steve Butabi (Will Ferrell)
A Night at the Roxbury

Ummmm . . . ummmm . . . Ladies and gentlemen . . . I'm sorry . . . As you probably have surmised by now . . . there will be no wedding. The bride . . . has had second thoughts . . . and has decided not to marry me . . . Most of you know me . . . Can you blame her?

Arthur (Dudley Moore)
Arthur

Dressing Up

You'll have to wait and see it. It's fierce . . . It has its own show.
Jennifer Hudson

The only reason he didn't get married in my husband's shoes is that his feet were larger.
Lady Biffen
on how Boris Johnson turned up with the wrong clothes and had to walk down the aisle in trousers and cufflinks borrowed from Tory MP John Biffen

Piper: Phoebe, let's not blow this out of proportion.
Phoebe: My wedding dress could double as a circus tent, I think things are already out of proportion.
Charmed

I can't explain why a bride buys her wedding dress, whereas a groom rents his tux.
Lou Holtz

Don't worry, Miss Bahmra. Our designs will make even these little
mosquito bites look like juicy, juicy mangoes!
Dressmaker
Bend It Like Beckham

Forty is the last age a woman can be photographed in a wedding dress
without the unintended Diane Arbus subtext.
Enid Frick

The modern bride dresses to kill,
and she usually cooks the same way.
Anon

My wife spent a fortune on a wedding dress.
Complete waste of money to my mind. She's worn it once.
I've worn it more than she has.
Mike Gunn

The mother of the bride . . . has a double whammy to contend with.
First, people are going to be checking her out to see how well-preserved
and well-dressed she is and second, they want to see what the bride is
going to look like in a few years' time
Helena Frith Powell

The market for wedding dresses is more often than not led by emotion
and aspiration rather than rational decisions and financial constraints.
Claire Birks

I want to look a bit covered-up and virginal. Pete knows what's
underneath, I suppose, but then again so does everyone else.
Katie Price

I can't believe I have to walk down the aisle in front of 200 people
looking like something you drink when you're nauseous!
Rachel (Jennifer Aniston)
Friends

She's insisting on keeping [her wedding dress] for ever. She said it
would be really romantic if when she dies she could be buried in it. I
said, "Well you better hope you die of some kind of wasting disease".
Mike Gunn

I started my day with a chipped tooth. My wedding planner snuck me
out to the dentist! Thank goodness it was fixed within the hour.
Hilary Duff

I don't know if I'd want Oompa Loompas on my nails while taking
photos, so I'm going to have wedding white nails.
Katy Perry

I'll try and get something silk to go with a diamond-encrusted tie. Then
that will leave Laura to get a wedding dress from Primark, or a bargain
basement shop like that.
Pearse O'Halloran

It can take years. One celebrity's dress we have been
working on for two years! We are doing three dresses for her and all
eight of her bridesmaids' dresses!

Hollywood wedding dress designer
Melissa Sweet

We are going to do the wedding naked –
all the families will be naked!
Russell Brand

Try to not get your dress dirty,
because you can wear it trick-or-treating.
Wendy Liebman

After the ceremony her dress is carefully, lovingly cleaned, folded,
sealed, wrapped in plastic, saved and preserved as an altar and shrine
for life. The groom's clothing is rented and has to be back to the shop
on Monday 'cos another guy needs it next weekend.
Rex Havens

I make the wedding dresses, in my special way,
I make them for those pretty girls, on their special day.
But sometimes I get angry and I make such a fuss,
When I lift up the dress and find the bride's got a penis.
Ryan Stiles
Weddings Hoedown on *Whose Line Is It Anyway?*

We spend so much money on these dresses that are terrible. And what do we get out of it? Nothing – a piece of chicken and a roll in the hay with her hillbilly cousin – no thank you. My family's very close; I can do that at home.

Chelsea Handler

It was great, but the entire bridal party was dressed in brown. It looked more like a shift meeting at UPS: "Do you promise to get this package there overnight?" "I do."

Howard Kremer

Samantha, we're looking at wedding gowns – could you please not talk about AIDS right now?

Charlotte York (Kristin Davis)
Sex and The City

You want pasta, you go to Little Italy.
You want wedding, you go Wang.

Anthony Marintino (Mario Cantone)
Sex and The City

Guest (sotto voce): Have you noticed that when there are two men in kilts at a wedding, you never see them talking to each other?

Overheard by
Miles Kington

A good idea is to put your wedding gown on early, so that the sweat stains can expand from your armpit areas and cover the entire gown, and thus be less noticeable.

Dave Barry

There are 1,400 gowns in this magazine and I've only seen 600 of them,
I need help.
Charlotte York (Kristin Davis)
Sex and The City

Chelsea wore a strapless gown by Vera Wang; her mother,
Secretary of State Hilary Clinton, wore something tasteful from the
Men's Warehouse.
Jimmy Kimmel

I'm a snow beast!
Toula Portokalos (Nia Vardalos)
seeing herself in her wedding gown for the first time, *My Big Fat Greek Wedding*

Stacey: I know it's [the dress] white, right. But who can honestly say,
hand on heart, they're a virgin these days?
Gavin and Stacey

Why do brides wear white? Because it's the most popular colour for
kitchen appliances.
–Anon

There was a time when no one would dare wear white to a wedding. It
was said to take away from the bride.
Christy James

The wedding was complete. Charlotte had something
old, something new, something borrowed and someone Samantha blew.
Carrie Bradshaw (Sarah Jessica Parker)
Sex and The City

I bought my best hat for my wedding. It was a real good hat – it
outlasted my marriage.
Bill McCoin

I will not be singing and don't expect
any track suits at my wedding.
Jane Lynch
(who plays aggressive cheerleading coach Sue Sylvester in *Glee*)

Karen : Why are wedding dresses funny?
Bride: Funny?
Karen: Yes, because when I asked my mummy and daddy in the car
would the bride would be wearing white they said "Yes"
and started giggling.
Outnumbered

My dad said I could wear some of my new stuff but my mum said
"He can't wear a tracksuit to a wedding". I'll never forget my dad's
reply: "It's still a suit".
Chris Ramsey

This time I'm going to be the bride. She got me these pink panties with
a big bow on them.
Billy Bob Thornton
on re-marrying Angelina Jolie

When didn't a bride have to hang on to a rather daft hat? . . .
But a lovely one nonetheless.

Nicholas Owen

on Camilla Parker-Bowles

When I wear latex onstage, I sweat. I could wring out those dresses –
and I don't want to do that at my wedding.

Katy Perry

Katie and me could go as Princess Leia and Darth Vader –
I'm up for that idea.

Alex Reid

considers a Star Wars-themed wedding

I knew that my princess needed her glass slippers and her castle.

Kevin Jonas

who gave his bride Danielle Deleasa a real pair of the
fairy-tale shoes before their wedding

Chelsea Clinton wore a dress designed by Vera Wang. You know,
usually when you hear the words Clinton and Wang in a sentence
together it has nothing to do with fashion.

Jimmy Kimmel

The bride was ravishing, as always, in white.
The groom wasn't bad either.

François Lebel

on Carla Bruni and Nicolas Sarkozy

Gwen: Perhaps Stacey doesn't want to get married in Essex.
What is she going to do here, totter down the aisle in a mini skirt and
white stilettos?
Pam: Shut it, you leek-munching sheep-shagger.
Gavin and Stacey

Pete: Why have I got to wear this stuff anyway?
It's horrible, it's itchy.
Ben: Because we're going to a wedding and everyone has to be as
uncomfortable as humanly possible. It's the law.
Outnumbered

Liv: My hair's blue! It's blue! I have blue hair!
I'm getting married in a week!
Hairdresser: Congratulations.
Bride Wars

I remember going to a wedding a few years ago and being horrified
that the woman in front of me wearing some kind of violet polyester
creation was the mother of the bride. I thought she was there to take
the church collection.
Helena Frith Powell

I couldn't believe the groom was married in rented shoes. You're
making a commitment for a lifetime and your shoes have to be back by
five-thirty.
Jerry Seinfeld

All I know is that I've ruled out wearing fairy wings.
When I was nine I wanted to get married in fairy wings, and now I
realize that's not cool any more.

Isla Fisher

(married to Sacha Baron Cohen)

And we were dressed from head to toe in love . . .
the only label that never goes out of style.

Carrie Bradshaw (Sarah Jessica Parker)

Sex and The City

Ceremony and Vows

Since Americans throw rice at weddings,
do Asians throw hamburgers?
Steven Wright

Women are still given away on their wedding day – we [men] should be
given away by our mums. We should be dragged down the aisle by the ear.
Hal Cruttenden

Pete: Right Ben. Little reminder: gravel . . . confetti. Only you seemed
to get the two a bit confused at your aunty Sandra's wedding, didn't
you. And when the priest says "Does anyone know any reason why
these people can't get married", no shouting out funny answers OK?
Ben: What, you mean like "She's a man?"
Outnumbered

Priest: I, Ross . . .
Ross: I, Ross . . .
Priest: take thee, Emily . . .
Ross: take thee, Rachel—
Friends

With all thy goods with thee I share . . .
Prince Charles
fluffs his wedding vows (married Diana Spencer)

The bride's family sat on this side, and the groom's family sat on that
side 'cos of the restraining order.
Wendy Liebman

Mine was "Girl I want to be with you all of the time, all day and all of
the night", and hers was "You are my sunshine, my only sunshine. You
make me happy when skies are grey".
Tim Minchin

Jennifer Aniston: I promise to always make your
favourite banana milkshake.
Brad Pitt: I vow to split the difference on the thermostat.

We ran out of classical music –
that's how long this wedding went on.
Richard Lewis

I've also always been fascinated by weddings . . . those surreal
performances . . . the knife inserted ritually into the virginal white cake
to reveal the dark fruity interior . . . that ugly pagan concept of the father
handing over his daughter to her new master.
David Gedge

A wedding is a funeral where you smell your own flowers.
Eddie Cantor

Wedding is destiny, and hanging likewise.
John Heywood

Weddings are giant Rorschach tests onto which everyone around you projects their fears, fantasies, and expectations – many of which they've been cultivating since the day you were born.
Susan Jane Gilman

All weddings are similar, but every marriage is different.
John Berger

Two TV aerials meet on a roof, fall in love, get married. The ceremony was rubbish but the reception was brilliant.
Tommy Cooper

My heart stopped when I first saw her. I kind of went blank, If you can imagine gasping for air, that's what I was doing. She looked stunning.
Tico Torres
(drummer in Bon Jovi) on seeing his bride Eva Herzigova coming down the aisle

If a bride has cold feet at the altar
And questions the groom's intentions
She better hope the best man wins.
Arthur Tugman

A man looks pretty small at a wedding, George. All those good women standing shoulder to shoulder, making sure that the knot's tied in a mighty public way.
Thornton Wilder

Vicar: Do you take this woman to be your wife?
Scouser: What if I do?
Harry Enfield's Television Programme

Dear Lord, forgive me for what I am about to, ah, say in this
magnificent place of worship . . . Bugger! Bugger! Bugger, bugger,
bugger, bugger!
Charles (Hugh Grant)
Four Weddings and a Funeral

I had a fairytale wedding – Grimm.
Marti Caine

If your kid is crying at a wedding or a funeral,
pinch their inner thigh.
Chad Daniels

He said as long as he doesn't have to pay for it again
he'd give away any bride.
Susan Dinelaor

I guess walking slow when getting married is because it gives you time
to maybe change your mind.
Virginia Cary Hudson

We need to alter the wedding vow. Till death do us part – or until you
become an inconvenience.
Carl Young

Marriage: a legal or religious ceremony by which two persons of the opposite sex solemnly agree to harass and spy on each other for ninety-nine years, or until death do them join.

Elbert Hubbard

Vicar: Do you solemnly swear to leave Liverpool at the earliest opportunity, live elsewhere, and spend the rest of your life going on about how great Liverpool is without ever returning?
Scouser: I do.

Harry Enfield's Television Programme

The Wedding March has a bit of a death march in it.

Brian May

There's nothing like a Catholic wedding to make you wish life had a fast forward button.

Daniel Chopin

I love seeing white people at Indian weddings cause they're always like, "Oh my God, what an amazing cultural experience. The colours – it's all so beautiful!" . . . then three hours later they're like "WHEN IS THIS GOING TO END, GOD, PLEASE, WHEN?"

Vijai Nathan

When the Wedding March sounds the resolute approach, the clock no longer ticks, it tolls the hour. The figures in the aisle are no longer individuals, they symbolize the human race.

Anne Morrow Lindbergh

How do you know you're at a redneck wedd
Everyone's sitting on the same side of the ch

Anon

People cry at weddings for the same reason they cry at happy endings:
because they so desperately want to believe in something they know is
not credible.

Margaret Atwood

"I am" is reportedly the shortest sentence in the English language.
Could it be that "I do" is the longest sentence?

George Carlin

He took the bride about the neck and kissed her lips with such a
clamorous smack that at the parting all the church did echo.

William Shakespeare

In olden times, sacrifices were made at the altar,
a practice that still continues.

Helen Rowland

The Wedding March always reminds me of the music played when
soldiers go into battle.

Heinrich Heine

When two people are under the influence of the most violent, most
insane, most delusive, and most transient of passions, they are required
to swear that they will remain in that excited, abnormal, and exhausting
condition continuously until death do them part.

George Bernard Shaw

I think weddings are sadder than funerals,
because they remind you of your own wedding. You can't be reminded
of your own funeral because it hasn't happened.
But weddings always make me cry.
Brendan Behan

A wedding is a ceremony at which two persons undertake to become
one, one undertakes to become nothing, and nothing undertakes to
become supportable.
Ambrose Bierce

I always cry at weddings, especially my own.
Humphrey Bogart

All weddings, except those with shotguns in evidence, are wonderful.
Liz Smith

I would like to keep my ceremony very small, very intimate, I don't
believe in an ostentatious wedding, because I want to save my money
for the divorce.
Dane Cook

Princess Diana got married to Prince Charles in a ceremony that lasted
longer than a number of major wars.
Dave Barry

The weather co-operated nicely; just as the vows were exchanged the sun set over our lake and it was just a special day and a wonderful day and we're mighty blessed.

George W. Bush
on daughter Jenna's wedding

If I get married again, I want a guy there with a drum to do rim shots during the vows.

Sam Kinison

Assistant Registrar: Oh dear. This is a bit embarrassing. I seem to have mislaid my pencil. Has any guest got one I could borrow?
Groom's stepfather: You can borrow mine, as long as you don't mind that it's from Disneyland.

Overheard by
Miles Kington

I wish them a long and happy life.
If it's as long as their wedding, I'm sure they'll be fine.

Michael Palin

For others who may not know this: when the preacher says, "You may kiss the bride", he's only speaking to the groom.

David Gunter

So many people still talk about it to this day;
"I can't believe you gave him a high-five". It's just something that we always did to each other backstage that we just carried out to the wedding itself.

Misty Haven

A limbo dancer married a locksmith yesterday . . .
the wedding was low-key.

Anon

Jeremy: Let me piss in that prayer bucker.
Mark: Prayer bucket? There's no such thing as . . .
that's just a bucket.

Peep Show

I tend to cry when I'm happy, and I did then.
And then Samantha started crying.

David Cameron

So I was sort of stood at the back and that, watching, and, er, I couldn't
hear what was going on, cos a woman was breastfeeding her baby . . . it
was slurping, and all that.

Karl Pilkington

I now pronounce you man and wife . . . well done.
You may now kiss the bride . . . nice one.

Rowan Atkinson
Priest

We get married every year. That's our thing.

Nick Cannon
on plans to renew wedding vows to Mariah Carey
a third time for their second anniversary

From a wedding or a christening nothing new is learnt, but funerals are different. A funeral or memorial service almost always teaches us things we never suspected about the dead.

Matthew Parris

Signing the register felt to me more dramatic than any of the stuff I had been sending up for years. Signing my biggest contract was like giving an autograph compared to it.

Roger Moore
(married Luisa Mattioli)

If I had to choose between going to a funeral or going to a wedding, I'd always choose a funeral because there's something so final about a wedding.

Miles Kington

Ben: Why has Jesus got that sad expression on his face?
Sue: Well he's being . . . crucified and it's making him feel sad.
Ben: He's got nails in his hands, he should be going Aaaaahhhh!

Outnumbered

The day of the wedding went like these things generally do, full of anxious moments interspersed with black comedy.

Janet Street-Porter

The Irish are often nervous about having the appropriate face for the occasion. They have to be happy at weddings, which is a strain, so they get depressed; they have to be sad at funerals, which is easy, so they get happy.

Peggy Noonan

The marriage got off to a bad start during the wedding service. The vicar said, "You may now kiss the bride." She replied, "Not now. I've got a headache."

Michael Bradley

Vicar, Rabbi, Priest

There's nothing more off-putting at a wedding than a priest with an enormous erection.

Charles (Hugh Grant)
Four Weddings and a Funeral

Most clergy I know prefer taking funerals to taking weddings and this isn't because we are essentially miserable or mawkish. Modern funerals, however painful, still have a beauty, a quiet dignity and a moral seriousness that is quite absent from many of the weddings that we get to take.

Rev Dr Giles Frasor
Canon Chancellor of St Paul's Cathedral

The vicar spoke like Brian Sewell. You could tell that he had utter contempt for the bride and groom ... Her nipples played at peekaboo with the bodice of her dress. The bridegroom's head was completely bald and covered in small cuts, having been shaved by drunken friends the night before. He chewed gum throughout the service.

Sue Townshend

I had to go to Pre-Cana class before I got married. That's when I had to go to a Catholic priest, and he was going to tell me how to live with a woman the rest of my life. Anybody see the irony in that? It's not like I'm marrying a 12-year-old Filipino boy.

Nick DiPaolo

A young attractive bride-to-be came up to me after the service and asked me just that question: "Father, what is the church's attitude towards fellatio?" And I replied, "Well, you know, Joanne, I'd like to tell you, but unfortunately, I don't know what fellatio is!" And so, she showed me. And ever since, whenever anyone has asked me the question "Father, what is the church's attitude towards fellatio?" I always reply, "Well, you know, I'd like to tell you . . . but unfortunately, I don't know what fellatio is!"

Rowan Atkinson
Priest

Every time I go to one of my friend's weddings, I'm sat on the table with the only other gay man, and we never have anything in common. It's always me who has to praise him for conducting such a beautiful service.

Paul Sinha

Too many modern weddings have just lost their way. I'd even say that they've become a threat to marriage itself.

Rev Dr Giles Fraser
Canon Chancellor of St Paul's Cathedral

At a Reconstructionist wedding,
the rabbi and her wife are both pregnant.

Anon

The Ring

Wedding rings are more than just symbols of eternity. They're magic curses made with backwards-speaking Latin.

Michael Loftus

Wedding rings: the world's smallest handcuffs.

Homer Simpson

I don't think it's fair – you get married, you give your wife a wedding ring. I think you should give her a mood ring. Oh, it may sound crass, but just check the colour when you come home. "Hi honey. Infernal red? Oh boy, I ain't getting laid, and I gotta cut the lawn, I know it."

Adam Ferrara

Ben: How much do wedding rings cost?
Pete: I mean it really depends, you know? I think you're supposed to spend like three months' pay on a ring.
Ben: Well, that'll be easy. I don't make any money.

Knocked Up

Cadence Flaherty: So, can I see the ring?
Steve Stifler: Nope. Promised to keep it safe.
It's not leaving my pocket.
Cadence Flaherty: Okay, Frodo.
American Pie: The Wedding

To me rings are special and exciting, but tattoos mean more than anything. They're for ever and ever. They profess our love.
Nick Cannon
(married Mariah Carey)

At our friends' wedding, just before Christmas we sang The 12 Days of Christmas . . . I got Five Gold Rings. Even though I can't sing, I went for it really loudly. The entire church turned and looked at me, which, of course, made me laugh. The bride and groom didn't find it funny, though.
Marcus Brigstocke

I've chosen my wedding ring large and heavy to continue for ever. But exactly because of that all the time that Dave and I have an argument I feel it like handcuffs, and on anger time I throw it in a basket. Poor Dave, he bought me three wedding rings already.
Carmen Miranda

Marriage requires a person to prepare four types of rings:
Engagement Ring, Wedding Ring, Suffering, Enduring.
Anon

Marriage: a ceremony in which rings are put on the finger of the lady and through the nose of the gentleman.
Herbert Spencer

Bridesmaids

My sister just got married.
I was the maid of debt in that little event.
Kathleen Madigan

To look beautiful at your wedding, take time to plan it. It took me a long time to find two ugly bridesmaids and a frumpy little flower girl.
Phyllis Diller

Our doggies are taking the bridesmaid roles. I was originally thinking little bow ties for them but instead they're going to each have flower collars.
Ayda Field
(married Robbie Williams)

It's time for me to boom boom with the bridesmaids, Finch f**ker, cuz I'm gonna hang out with my wang out, and I'm gonna rock out with my cock out!
Steve Stifler (Seann William Scott)
American Pie: The Wedding

I don't know which was worse, the cost of the bridesmaid dress or
having to wear it.
Debbie Etchings

Why would your friends make you wear an ugly dress? Because it's their
wedding, not yours. My friends weren't even nice. They're like, "Could
the dress show more back fat? Let's get these tighter."
Megan Mooney

If I can't get drunk at a wedding and sleep with a bridesmaid then I
don't want to go.
Lloyd Langford

A happy bridesmaid makes a happy bride.
Tennyson

Jane: God, Casey, can't you keep it in your pants for one wedding?
Casey: Are you kidding? The only reason to wear this monstrous dress
is so that some drunken groomsman can rip it to shreds with his teeth.
27 Dresses

Oh, sweetie, you are my second cousin's best friend, of course you're at
the very top of my maid of honour list, honestly . . . Carla . . . Caitlyn?
Emma (Anne Hathaway)
Bride Wars

The other bridesmaid's got three pets. Can we get one?
Karen
Outnumbered

Speeches and Toasts

Dad has only said "I'm so proud of you" the once. It was on my wedding day and we were in the house, just me and him, waiting for the car to pick us up. It was followed by a lot of coughing and changing the subject. But it was totally sincere and from the heart.

Lorraine Kelly

From those to whom much is given, much is expected.

Mary Gates

mother of Bill Gates, in a letter to Melinda before the wedding

Opening speaker: We have visitors here from as far away as Hong Kong, Sweden, South Africa and Bournemouth.

Overheard by
Miles Kington

A tip for grooms: if you want to practise your lines, do so in the privacy of your hotel room, rather than, as I did, muttering them to yourself during the main course, or people will tend to show concern.

Michael Deacon

You know I wasn't even invited to this wedding.
Brooke Shields' mother, Teri
opens her wedding speech

Carol's family have always had their doubts about me so first of all let me explain why I'm naked.
Frankie Boyle
"Bad Things to Say at a Wedding", *Mock The Week*

But here's the thing: however stammeringly hopeless your speech, your guests will laugh kindly and applaud. As they should, of course, seeing as you've paid for their dinner.
Michael Deacon

Maria: Greek women, we may be lambs in the kitchen, but we are tigers in the bedroom.
Toula: Eww. Please let that be the end of your speech.
My Big Fat Greek Wedding

As far as I'm concerned, my daughter could not have chosen a more delightful, charming, witty, responsible, wealthy, let's not deny it, well-placed, good-looking and fertile young man than Martin as her husband. And I therefore ask the question, "Why the hell did she marry Gerald instead?"
Rowan Atkinson
Father Of The Bride Speech

Speech highlights include my best man asking any women who hd a key to my house to return it immediately, causing half the women at the reception to approach my table and plonk a key in front of me. The implication was that I was some kind of womaniser, although when my pal Tim then got up, that proved that I'm not just all about the ladies. When the bride's mum got up to return a key too . . .

Paul Kerensa

It's all . . . it's all starting to come back to me now . . . huh-huh, erm . . . and I . . . just to know that their marriage will be as happy and satisfying as I when I paid off those two prostitutes earlier this morning . . . cheers!

Rowan Atkinson
Best Man Speech

Now this wedding today is costing me a fortune and I would like to call upon the chef to come out and face us. Today was the first time I saw roast beef glowing in the dark.

Brendan Grace
as Father of the Bride

I've never seen my sister this happy, Ian. If you hurt her, I'll kill you and make it look like an accident.

Nick (Louis Mandylor)
My Big Fat Greek Wedding

I started with the words, "Jasper Carrott as a warm-up man . . . that's not a bad gig!"

Owain Yeoman
on his wedding speech to Carrot's daughter Lucy Davis

Now it's my job to tell some amusing stories about Gavin so first of all
for a kick-off, he's a hermaphrodite.

Frankie Boyle

"Bad Things to Say at a Wedding", *Mock The Week*

Dear Stacey, if you are reading this, it must be your wedding day. But if
it isn't, and Bryn has just left it lying around, then tell him he's a waste
of space and could never be trusted to do anything properly.

Bryn (Rob Brydon)

reads a letter from Stacey's dead father on her wedding day, *Gavin and Stacey*

I remember when she first came to me and she said that she wanted
to get married. I said "is it someone you know?" It turned out to be
someone we all know.

Brendan Grace

as Father of the Bride

I've got two things to announce to you of the greatest importance. The
first is that the Grand National was won by Hedgehunter. The second
is to say to you that despite Becher's Brook and The Chair and all kinds
of other terrible obstacles my son has come through and I'm very proud
and wish them well.

Queen Elizabeth II

at the wedding of Prince Charles and Camilla Parker-Bowles

God bless my parents, God bless my family, God bless my friends, God
bless my beloved wife. But damn the British Press.

Prince Charles

(married Camilla Parker-Bowles)

So he came around to my house . . . and he said,
"I'd like to marry your daughter."
I said, "Have you seen her mother?"
He said, "I have, but I'd sooner marry your daughter."

Brendan Grace
as Father of the Bride

I'd like to thank you for your presence
and thank you for your presents.

Steve Harris's
brief wedding speech

You were so calm and composed during the service
and said your words with such conviction that I knew it was
all right . . . I can see that you are sublimely happy with
Philip, which is right, but 'Don't forget us' is the wish of
your ever loving and devoted papa.

Note to Elizabeth II from her father
King George VI

Sliocht sleachta ar shliocht bhur sleachta
(May your children's children have children).

Gaelic toast

May you never lie, cheat or drink. But if you must lie, lie with each other. And if you must cheat, cheat death. And if you must drink, drink with us for we all love you and wish you both the love and happiness which you deserve.

May all your ups and downs be between the sheets.

To our wives and lovers – may they never meet!

Here's a toast to your new bride who has everything a girl could want in her life, except for good taste in men.

All Anon

Photos and Videos

Peter Andre might look smug in all his wedding pictures, but I'd just like to remind him that, as a Playboy reader, I have seen his wife's minge. He hasn't seen my wife's, so who's had the last laugh?

'P.', Leeds
Viz Letters

Their decision to marry has not been made with any pre-conceived commercial plan or media deal in place, and their reason for getting married is purely down to their love for each other.

Katie Price and Alex Reid's publicist
after the couple seal a £1 million deal for exclusive pictures of their wedding.

Eyes down. Don't smile. Indian bride never smiles. You'll ruin the bloody video!

Wedding videographer
Bend It Like Beckham

You'll want to have lots of photographs of your wedding to show to your family and friends, who will have been unable to see the actual ceremony because the photographer was always in the way.

Dave Barry

Every time I look at my wedding photos I think: "Why on earth did I wear my hair up?" The only day of my life when I arranged for my hair to be sprayed into a sculpted mound ,and I've spent the past 11 years lamenting it.

Rowan Pelling

Our dog died from licking our wedding picture.

Phyllis Diller

I wanted to look good for my wedding pictures. You might be looking at those things for four or five years.

Tom Arnold

They put these one-time use cameras out on the tables. I thought that was a great idea – 'til they got them pictures back, realized only them little bad kids had the cameras. They're going through hundreds of pictures like, "Oh, here's another one of the cat's butt".

Clinton Jackson

We married when I was 40. I was beginning to think it would never happen. In all the wedding pictures, I'm grinning like an idiot.

Alan Davies

I really did put up all my wedding pictures on my website. And I swear to you, my wedding pictures got downloaded just as much as my bikini pictures.

Cindy Margolis

Which of us did not look at the pictures from the Beckhams' wedding and, like Eliot's eternal Footman, 'snicker'? We had a right to: it was hilarious and quite mind-bogglingly vulgar.

Simon Barnes

You sacrificed an hour of perfectly good drinking time so he could get some nice angles of you on the swing, under the weeping willow tree in the churchyard. And where's the video now? I bet half of you don't even know.

Jeremy Clarkson

The Cake

Barbara: Two hundred pounds.
Denise: How many tiers is that?
Jim: There'll be plenty of bloody tears if it's two hundred pounds.
The Royle Family

Now let's cut the stupid cake because I know the fat guy's gonna have a
heart attack if we don't eat again soon.
Robbie (Adam Sandler)
The Wedding Singer

It was in the size and shape of – how can I put this politely? –
a pair of boobs.
Emma Thompson
on the wedding cake that was supposed to evoke the Scottish hills

— So, are you ready to go? Have they cut the cake yet?
— I don't know, but I can tell you how it turns out.
Sex and The City

The funniest moment was when Matt [Lucas] came in. He'd taken all the trouble to bring a wig and costume and brought in the cake dressed up as his Little Britain character. It brought a huge cheer.

Ronnie Corbett
on the wedding of David Walliams and Lara Stone

He made them put about four or five bottles of brandy in that cake. Ozzy ate it – he ate the whole cake – and was laid out ... He never made it into the bedroom on our wedding night.

Sharon Osbourne

I've never liked wedding cake due to the amount of icing, but then imagine a wedding cake without it: just a dark, stodgy, horrible, dry sponge ... Maybe blood cake would look better with icing though.

Karl Pilkington

In all of the wedding cake, hope is the sweetest of plums.

Douglas Jerrold

The most dangerous food is wedding cake.

James Thurber

What food sucks eighty per cent of the sex drive from a woman? Wedding cake.

Anon

Food and Drink

Whoever eats anything at a wedding luncheon?
They make the food out of papier mâché. My salad has been used
four or five times this week.
Peter Ruric

You can always spot the father of the bride – he's the one signing over
his retirement fund to the caterer.
Joe Hickman

Groom's stepfather: What on earth is this on my plate?
Not a rissole, I hope.
Waitress: No, sir. It's a Portobello mushroom.

Overheard by
Miles Kington

Guest: Is the bar meant to be Hawaiian?
Or do they have ukulele evening classes?

Overheard by
Miles Kington

Vol-au-vents, chicken legs, cheese cake . . . vol-au-vents, again, chicken legs, cheese cake – that's all there is, same food repeated. One table and a shit load of mirrors, that's the wedding buffet.

Peter Kay

The meal can be anything you like. The best thing you can say about wedding food is that it doesn't taste like wedding food.

Bee Wilson

I was a beer bride. I don't have one picture of me without a beer in my hand. It was a great wedding   and an amazing divorce. So it all worked out fine.

Kate Hudson

We thought it was a bad idea you guys got married, but we didn't feel like we could say anything because it was open bar.

Megan Mooney

Triangular sandwiches taste better than square ones.

Peter Kay

A wedding is a sacrament . . . a joyous celebration of love and commitment. In Utopia. In the real world . . . it's an excuse to drink excessively and say things you shouldn't say.

Nick Mercer (Dermot Mulroney)
The Wedding Date

I keep explaining to Damian that actors are coming. They will eat and drink everything in sight. His lot are in advertising so you can imagine it is going to be a very boozy wedding.

Amanda Redman

People feel anxious when they are about to wed. In the absence of clear traditions they fall back on clichés: hence the ubiquitous rubbery shrimp platters that grace weddings in America, or the poached salmon and cucumber salad that always used to be served here.

Bee Wilson

Pete: Ben, Ben, you can't dip sardines in the chocolate fountain.
Ben: Yes you can, look.
Karen: See, he can.

Outnumbered

We missed you at the wedding. It was really classy.
We had a Styx cover band, and a nacho fountain.
Check it, it was a nacho fountain.

Cal Naughton, Jr. (John C. Reilly)
Talladega Nights

The best time to drink champagne is not when somebody has a 21st birthday, or a wedding, or has passed an exam (though it may work well at all those times), but when one is thirsty.

Simon Heffer

An Irish wedding is a tame thing to an Irish funeral.

Mary Deasy

Here, have some gum, it'll stop that gurning.

Guest to Kate Moss

at wedding

Song and Dance

'Hi Ho Silver Lining' has ruined more wedding receptions than Phil
[Jupitus] being first in line at the buffet.
Mark Lamarr

No matter what kind of music you ask them to play, your
wedding band will play it in such a way that it sounds like
'New York, New York'.
Dave Barry

Joy Behar just cannot let go of the fact that Elton John performed at
my wedding. She just can't let go of this. It's like a box of old tampons.
She just can't get rid of it.
Rush Limbaugh

The Wedding Dance is a timeless ritual . . . surrounded by a
group of family and friends – watching, smiling, taking bets on how
long it's going to last. All you have is each other and whatever skills you
acquire today.
Dance Instructor
The Wedding Date

There's always some cousin in his thirties blind drunk who still reckons
he can break-dance.
Peter Kay

My wedding didn't go well. For our first dance, my bride chose 'I Still
Haven't Found What I'm Looking For'.
Paul Kerensa

At 18, I married a vacuum cleaner salesman with a lazy eye. Our
wedding song was "Two Out of Three Ain't Bad" by Meatloaf.
Carmen Stockton

I love Robbie Williams; I think he's a great entertainer; 'Angels' was the
first dance at my wedding and anyone who criticises him is just jealous.
Who am I? I'm an idiot.
Simon Amstell

I love DJs at weddings, DJs that talk all night and you can't understand
a word they say.
Peter Kay

My wife and I had Morris dancers at our wedding too in
November, the Forest of Dean Morris Men, who did this amazing
thing with a giant stag-headed man.
Stewart Lee

Father of the Bride: Hey, buddy, I'm not paying you to share your thoughts on life. I'm paying you to sing.

Robbie: Well, I have a microphone and you don't, SO YOU WILL LISTEN TO EVERY DAMN WORD I HAVE TO SAY!!

The Wedding Singer

And don't get me started on wedding disco DJs, and the way they keep shouting over the microphone . . . calling everyone who isn't dancing "boooooring" . . . Yeah, thanks for that. Draw attention to me, why don't you?

Stephen Fry

The DJ adhered to the rule of occasion
Dancing Queen
Shoop Shoop Song
You're the One That I Want
They're the ones that they want

Half Man, Half Biscuit
"I Went to a Wedding"

He's a snapper. He just sways back and forth and snaps his finger.

Kellie Pickler
(married Kyle Jacobs)

[Write down] everything you wanna say to Portia and everything you wanna say to Ellen . . . and I'll put it to music and it'll be amazing.

Justin Timberlake
congratulates Ellen DeGeneres and Portia De Rossi

I'd love to perform with Cheryl [Cole] and I think a great time to do it would be at Simon's [Cowell] wedding – what else do you get the man who has everything?"

Katy Perry

Grandmas always go early.
"Sandra, grandma's going. Come say goodbye. It's ten to eight . . . go on grandma, you get home, get a shave."

Peter Kay

Have you ever noticed how every time a coalition air strike goes astray in Iraq, it always manages to hit a wedding party?

Richard Littlejohn

Gifts

Don't get divorced or I want my juicer back.
Jim Jeffries

When we got married, we had our wedding list at Bloomingdale's, because you can exchange everything for cash. Each place-setting kept me in beer money for three months.
Gary Barkin

They didn't give a wedding list, but the last thing I got him –
he's a very difficult man to get presents for – was some coffee from Cambodian weasel vomit.
Stephen Fry
on his wedding gift to Prince Charles and Camilla

Whenever people got married, she would give as a wedding present a Kenwood mixer and the Kama Sutra, saying both would prove useful.
Clarissa Dickson Wright
on her mother

Supermarkets and electrical retailers have reported a run on old-style 100 watt bulbs, as people stockpile them for decades to come. And as these lightbulbs become rarer, they'll become increasingly valuable. Lightbulbs might be given as wedding gifts or anniversary presents.

Natalie Haynes

George: Any way she's gonna believe it actually came from me?
Jane: Maybe. I wrapped it like a car ran over it.
George: Nice touch.

27 Dresses

I was going to get them a dinner service, but I'm not actually convinced the marriage would last, so I settled for two picnic baskets.

Victoria Wood

That's a curious tradition, the wedding list, isn't it? "Buy us presents but don't use your imagination, we'll have none of that".

Ed Byrne

Royalty, when they marry, either get very small things, like exquisitely constructed clockwork eggs, or large, bulky items, like duchesses.

Terry Pratchett

I went to the store with my wife 'cos we got a gift card from our wedding, and I went with her thinking I could help spend some of the money on the gift card. Rookie move – apparently, my name is just on there for decoration.

John Heffron

You can't have everything you want on a wedding list. Certain things don't go. Xbox 360 games don't go on a wedding list . . . they can go on the list but they'll have mysteriously disappeared . . . replaced by something called a soup tureen.

Ed Byrne

The only thing harder than choosing a spot for your wedding when you hate weddings is choosing a wedding gift for your friend who hates weddings.

Carrie Bradshaw (Sarah Jessica Parker)
Sex and The City

So you wound up with Apollo.
If he's sometimes hard to swallow . . .
Use this.

Inscription on a silver cup, the wedding gift from

Paul Newman
to his bride Joanne Woodward

Wedding Night

I'm all for trial marriages. The wedding of two virgins
starts off with a huge handicap.
Sean Connery

Nurse Gladys Emmanuel: What are your meringues like?
Arkwright: I'm not telling you till after we're married.
Open All Hours

I'd hate to be next door to her on her wedding night.
Peter Ustinov
on Monica Seles

Getting married for sex is like buying a 747 for the free peanuts.
Jeff Foxworthy

To be honest about it, sex was not worth the wait. After we did it, I was
kind of like, "That's it?"
Kevin Jonas
on having sex for the first time on his honeymoon

I have no boobs whatsoever. On my wedding night my husband said, "Let me help you with those buttons," and I told him, "I'm completely naked."

Joan Rivers

On the negative side, there is the wedding night, during which the bride must pay the piper, so to speak, by facing for the first time the terrible experience of sex.

Ruth Smythers
Instruction and Advice for the Young Bride, 1894

Before I met my wife, I had virtually no experience. I remember on our wedding night, I tried to inflate her.

Jonathan Katz

According to a new study, Southerners are much more likely to have sex on their wedding night than other people. That makes sense – you're always going to be more comfortable with a relative.

Jay Leno

Elton John was paid $1 million to perform at Rush Limbaugh's wedding. Then Rush had to pay his wife twice that to perform on the wedding night.

Jay Leno

Five things not to say on your wedding night
1. You woke me up for that?
2. Try not to leave any stains, okay?
3. I think you have it on backwards.
4. When is this supposed to feel good?
5. I have a confession . . .

Anon

There was blood, because I had extremely sensitive skin,
and I told him, "Don't touch me". And I just lay on the bed.
That was our wedding night.

Joan Collins

on failing to consummate her fifth marriage after the maid of honour
left her bleeding when removing tape fixing down her bra

Some young women actually anticipate the wedding night ordeal with
curiosity and pleasure! Beware such an attitude! A selfish and sensual
husband can easily take advantage of such a bride.

Ruth Smythers

Instruction and Advice for the Young Bride, 1894

There's a beautiful spiritual meaning . . . when an Indian woman gets
married she's supposed to bring a dowry with her to the wedding, an
investment, right? The night of the wedding her husband scratches the
dot to see if he's won a seven-eleven, a motel or a gas station.

Dalia McPhee

Bride: Darling, I must confess, I used to be a hooker.
Groom: That's OK. Besides, I find it quite erotic. Tell me more.
Bride: My name was Nigel and I played for Wigan.

Anon

Honeymooners
and Newlyweds

Lee Nelson: You look like a married man . . . What is, like, the best
thing about the marriage?
Audience member: The first few hours.
Lee Nelson's Well Good Show

My mother once told me that if a married couple puts a penny in a pot
for every time they make love in the first year, and takes a penny out
every time after that, they'll never get all the pennies out of the pot.
Armistead Maupin

Pity all newlyweds. She cooks something nice for him, and he brings
her flowers, and they kiss and think: How easy marriage is.
Mignon McLaughlin

You learn a lot about your spouse in the first year of marriage, man. I
found out I could not take my wife to a wedding that was
better than ours.
Cleto Rodriguez

We've been together a year, but I feel like it's been a lot longer because of all the crap that's happened to us.

Alex Reid
Alan Carr: Chatty Man

Guess the first thing we did after we staggered into our bridal suite. No, not that. The answer: we fumbled our way on to Facebook, via our respective mobile phones, in order to update our "relationship status" from "engaged" to "married".

Michael Deacon

I told him I would marry him on the condition that nothing would change. But when I woke up on the morning after the wedding I realised everything had changed and I loved it. I felt totally and utterly different.

Helen Mirren
(married Taylor Hackford)

Nothing is to me more distasteful than that entire complacency and satisfaction which beam in the countenances of a new-married couple.

Charles Lamb

I was like any new bride, who said, "I'm going to cook for my man". In fact, once I started a small kitchen fire in a pan. Smoke was pouring from the pan, and I got really scared.

Catherine Zeta Jones

The wedding and the honeymoon are probably the furthest thing from marriage.

Joseph Simmons

Next to hot chicken soup, a tattoo of an anchor on your chest, and penicillin, I consider a honeymoon one of the most overrated events in the world.
Erma Bombeck

We went to Mexico on our honeymoon, and spent the entire two weeks in bed. I had dysentery.
Woody Allen

The first year of marriage is like wet cement – the impressions made in it are much harder to change once it has set.
Robert Wolgemuth

The only thing worse than a smug married couple: lots of smug married couples.
Bridget Jones (Renée Zellweger)
Bridget Jones's Diary

I was disappointed in Niagara . . . Every American bride is taken there, and the sight of the stupendous waterfall must be one of the earliest, if not the keenest, disappointments in American married life.
Oscar Wilde

The day after that wedding night I found that a distance of a thousand miles, abyss and discovery and irremediable metamorphosis, separated me from the day before.
Colette

My sister started to smell trouble when, on the second day of her honeymoon, the groom started asking for separate cheques.

Wendy Morgan

The honeymoon is over when he phones to say he'll be late for supper and she's already left a note that it's in the refrigerator.

Bill Lawrence

We're eating DiGiorno's pizza, getting in that tanning oven every once in a while, it's great . . . It's gonna look like we're on that private jet. We're gonna save that 30 grand, you know?

Pete Wentz
on honeymoon with Ashlee Simpson

Honeymoon: a short period of doting between dating and debting.

Ray Bandy

It's time to get cracking on a honeymoon, baby – bring it on!

Katie Price
moments before heading to a strip club with Alex Reid

What do you have against honeymoons?
It's basically sex with room service.

Samantha Jones (Kim Cattrall)
Sex and The City

When the honeymoon is over a man discovers his wife isn't an angel, so he quits posing as a saint.

Anon

We're not planning a honeymoon.
We go on a honeymoon every other week.

John Travolta
(married Kelly Preston)

The honeymoon is over when she starts wondering what happened to the man she married, and he starts wondering what happened to the girl he didn't.

Anon

We had this terrible honeymoon at the Seven Sacred Pools in Maui, this gorgeous scene, and all I could do was smell the rotten mangoes . . . Thank God she didn't cut me loose, 'cos I was miserable to be around, but I finally got with the programme.

Jeff Bridges
(m. Susan Geston)

People take shorter honeymoons nowadays,
but they take them more often.

Anon

You know your marriage isn't off to a good start when your new bride asks, "Have you considered suicide?" So went the eight-day union of Dennis Hopper and Michelle Phillips.

Kat Giantis

Tom and I will always be in our honeymoon phase.

Katie Holmes

The first year of marriage, the man speaks and the woman listens. In the second year, the woman speaks and the man listens. In the third year, they both speak and the neighbours listen.

Anon

Never tell a secret to a bride or a groom; wait until they have been married longer.

Edgar Watson Howe

Marriage is like a phone call in the night:
first the ring, and then you wake up.

Evelyn Hendrickson

Gay Weddings

I think gay marriage is something that should
be between a man and a woman.
Arnold Schwarzenegger

Amazing news about Prop 8 being overturned. Now *The Sun* can make
up engagement stories about everyone!
Eli Roth
tweeting about the overturning of California's ban on same-sex marriages

And then there was the incredible irony that it took place in Middle
Temple underneath a portrait of Sir Edward Carson, the man who
prosecuted Oscar Wilde. So when I did my little speech the first thing I
did was flick him two fingers. "This one's for Oscar".
Mark Gatiss

They are preserving the sanctity of marriage, so that two gay men
who've been together for 25 years can't get married, but a guy can still
get drunk in Vegas and marry a hooker at the Elvis chapel!
Lea Delaria

If we can take a billion dollars to put a man on the moon, I think it's
OK to send two men on honeymoon if they are willing to register for
a billion dollars of gifts at Pottery Barn. This is not about civil rights
people, it's about the economy.

Mark Day

No one has asked me to marry them, sadly. I am all for civil
partnerships, but I do hope that there won't be a spate of silly Soho
queens waltzing down the aisle a week after they've met.

Julian Clary

I can't bear other people's weddings – it is a waste of a whole Saturday
. . . One of the nice things about being gay used to be that one was
spared the ceremonial baggage of marriage.

Matthew Parris

We should all have the right to marry whomever we wish, whether it
be male or female. That's what the 14th Amendment provides: equal
protection of the law.

Joseph Hansen

Nowadays only the gay people get married in LA.
Straight people don't bother any more.

Craig Chester

Gay people getting married is like retarded people getting together
to give each other PhDs. It doesn't make them smarter, and it doesn't
make us married.

Dan Savage

Legalized same-sex marriage has prompted a new slogan, "We're here, we're queer and we're registered at Williams-Sonoma."

Craig Kilborn

I'm gay, so why would I want to get married?
I'd prefer my sex life to continue.

Scott Capurro

Here's how I feel about gay marriage. I don't understand why people care whether you marry a man or a woman. 'Cos if you've ever seen a couple over 65, it is very hard to tell who is who.

Mo Mandel

"Now if your neighbour marries a box turtle, that doesn't affect your everyday life. But that doesn't mean it's right." I think it's pretty safe to assume that, at one point or another, Senator John Cornyn has thought about making love to a box turtle. I'm sorry, but that's not the first animal you jump to when you're writing that analogy.

Aziz Ansari

Minister: Gay, civil or religious?
Chuck: Religious. I'm Jewish, I don't want to piss my mother off.
Larry: I'm Catholic, I don't want to piss Mel Gibson off.

I Now Pronounce You Chuck and Larry

I think all gay guys should . . . have to get married. They should have to adopt kids because, actually, I'm getting tired of their happy-go-lucky lifestyle . . . I could look good in denim short shorts and combat boots too, if I had all day to do leg presses at the gym.

Greg Giraldo

Governor Schwarzenegger says this is not the proper venue to express gay sexuality, but try the locker room at Gold's Gym.

Bill Maher

I say no to gay marriage. It'll end up leading to gay divorce, and that'll be bitchy.

Jimmy Carr

The Bush administration renewed its call for a constitutional amendment to ban gay marriage. So I guess they feel the only time that guys should be on top of each other naked is in an Iraqi prison.

Jay Leno

Governor Schwarzenegger has come out against gay marriage and then he went back to slathering body oil all over his muscles in front of other guys.

Craig Kilborn

If the last two days are any indication, the race for the White House will be pretty much decided by whether two middle-aged women can open a joint checking account.

Jon Stewart

Our governor here has weighed in on the San Francisco situation. He said he wants them to stop the gay marriages going on up there, but he said that he still supports same-sex groping.

Bill Maher

President Bush said he was "troubled" by gay people getting married in San Francisco. He said on important issues like this the people should make the decision, not judges. Unless of course we're choosing a president – then he prefers judges.

Jay Leno

Celebrity Weddings

Miquita: So was it the happiest day of your life?
Matt Lucas (as Cheryl Cole): When the cheque for a million pounds
arrived, yes, certainly it was.
Rock Profile

On the face of it the wedding of Jade Goody and Jack Tweed was every
single little thing every right-thinking man and woman in this country
has come to loathe – the very recrudescence of the canker that infests
the social body.
Will Self

Jordan's got no celeb mates so she's paying them to go to her wedding.
Jodie Marsh

Who thought there would be two people who were too downmarket to
get married in Vegas?
David Walliams
on the wedding of Katie Price and Alex Reid

It's never less than 100,000 dollars up to half a million, depending on who they are or what it is . . . In the case of Donald Trump and Melania, the entire theme was white flowers. So for that week I bought out every single flower market in NYC.

Celebrity florist
Preston Bailey

I was watching everyone else enjoying themselves and having a fantastic time, and I couldn't help wishing that I was too.

Katie Price
on her wedding to Peter Andre

It will have a first dance, it will have all of them things, like anything else. It's no more interesting or no less spectacular than any marriage of anybody, so it's very beautiful and incredible and wonderful, but it's also utterly mundane.

Russell Brand

Liz Hurley's long-haul wedding has produced a carbon footprint so large that it would take the average British couple more than 10 years to contribute as much to heating up the planet as she and Arun Nayar have done in little over a week.

Geoffrey Lean and Rachel Beebe

Apart from the last-minute wedding in Vegas,
Alex has never been married.

Narrator
Katie & Alex: For Better, For Worse

It was a secret ceremony with just *The Sun, The Star,
The Mirror, OK, Hello, Grazia, Heat, Take a Break, TV Quick*
and *Puzzler* magazine present.

Jimmy Carr
on the wedding of Katie Price and Alex Reid

I want to make our wedding just about me and her loving
each other and we're getting married in front of our friends and
family and keeping it normal. So it ain't selling the pictures, ain't doing
no pre-nup.

Russell Brand

They say, instead of throwing rice, throw Vicodin.

Bill Maher
on Rush Limbaugh's wedding

You should not make a deal with a funeral parlour to get publicity, and
it's very bad taste to get publicity for a wedding.

Letitia Baldrige

The monumental fuss over the Clinton-Marc Mezvinsky nuptials
. . . proves one thing beyond doubt. In the unofficial monarchical
successions of the US, the Kennedys are dead, long live the Clintons.

Rupert Cornwell

The groom's face, pursed and red as a baboon's bottom, was the result,
he proudly declared, of "all the surgery. I'm all sewn up at the back."

Jemima Lewis
on the wedding of David Van Day and Sue Moxley

When I met Alex, I had no idea that one day he'd be the man I'd marry. Largely because at that stage he was yet to show any signs of winning a popular reality television series.

Katie Price (Michael Deacon)

The happy couple were surrounded by several hundred guests under an anti-terrorist no-fly zone that extended 30 miles.

Guy Adams

on the wedding of Chelsea Clinton and Marc Mezvinsky

At an actress's wedding reception, I was asked to eat with the kitchen staff as it was felt that nobody should know that the magazine was paying the couple £40,000 for the privilege of covering the event.

Clair Woodward

deputy editor of *OK!* magazine

They didn't write their own vows, but they did do some colouring in.

David Walliams

on the wedding of Katie Price and Alex Reid

We've been talking about doing a bigger wedding on our first anniversary. And maybe another one every year.

Mariah Carey

(married Nick Cannon)

The inside is tackier than Anthea Turner's wedding and you don't want to think what would happen if it bumped into a lamppost.

Jeremy Clarkson

reviewing the Perodua Kelisa 1.0 GXi

It is a complete joke . . . my response at the time, it's almost like the shock when you watch *Independence Day* and Will Smith goes outside and he looks at the paper and then he looks up and he sees a UFO.

Peter Andre

on his ex-wife Katie Price's wedding to Alex Reid.

We've decided that after we get married, we're not going to talk about our relationship any more because it's, like, we're married, so we're married. What more can I say?

Katy Perry

In Hollywood, brides keep the bouquets and throw away the groom.

Groucho Marx

There's a lot more pressure with celebrity weddings. You have to please not just the bride, but the stylist, the publicist, the manager, etc.

Hollywood wedding dress designer
Melissa Sweet

In the end, the only celebrities who made the effort to attend former glamour model Katie Price's wedding were former glamour model Melinda Messenger ('looking summery') and ahem former glamour model Danielle Lloyd.

Craig Brown

The bride, resplendent in a satin gown from Lakeside Shopping Centre, was given away by "Dr Khan, who does my Botox."

Jemima Lewis

on the wedding of David Van Day and Sue Moxley

There's no taboo about not really getting married
on your wedding day anymore.
Carley Roney

My husband and I didn't sign a pre-nuptial agreement.
We signed a mutual suicide pact.
Roseanne Barr

I didn't really understand my pre-nup but it was written in Vietnamese
by a sobbing father.
Jimmy Carr

We have the greatest pre-nuptial agreement in the world.
It's called love.
Gene Perret

You know, me and Ashleeeaaaah have to make time because
Ashleeeaaaah is a footballer and he's often playing away.
Matt Lucas (as Cheryl Cole)
Rock Profile

You need to create something that is so uniquely different
that it has truly never been seen before. Also we constantly bear in
mind how things will photograph for a magazine, the approach is
entirely different.

Celebrity florist
Preston Bailey

Tom Cruise has a freaky marriage. I reckon if you went round there for dinner she would have written "GET HELP" in the peas.

Frankie Boyle

The constitutionalist Walter Bagehot once said that a royal wedding is a brilliant edition of an everyday fact. One might say that a celebrity wedding is a grotesque edition of an everyday fact. And that's why we love them so.

Craig Brown

I loved it, pet, and of course they pay you extra for each celebrity that turns up. Posh and Becks we got twenty grand, Frank Lampard ten grand, Nicola [Roberts] they gave us a bag of Doritos and a guacamole dip.

Matt Lucas (as Cheryl Cole)
Rock Profile

Breaking Up

Ah, yes, "divorce". From the Latin for "having your genitals torn off through your wallet".
Robin Williams

Since the split with Peter Andre, Jordan has apparently hit the bottle and isn't eating properly. At least she's able to carry on as normal.
Frankie Boyle

You never truly know a woman until you meet her in court.
Anon

I can honestly say that life is fantastic now. I'm so happy that all the mess I used to have to deal with is not my mess any more.
Patsy Kensit
on her marriage breakup with Liam Gallagher

Having a wedding without mentioning divorce is like sending someone to war without mentioning that people are going to get killed.
Richard Curtis

Marriage is a conspiracy from Tiffany, florists, the diamond industry, and Christian fundamentalists. The only thing good about it is the diamond ring, the wedding gifts, and the honeymoon.

Suzanne Finnamore
Split: A Memoir of Divorce

Diamonds never leave you – men do!
Shirley Bassey

I can't for the life of me understand why people keep insisting that marriage is doomed. All five of mine worked out.
Peter de Vries

In Britain two out of three marriages end in divorce.
The other one ends in murder.
Jeff Green

Initially, I thought we had a chance, and we tried really hard. I felt stupid as more things were revealed – how could I not have known anything? The word 'betrayal' isn't strong enough.
Elin Nordegren
(married Tiger Woods)

We kind of rushed into it because we were so enamoured with each other, which is kind of narcissistic because we were one and the same.
Peaches Geldof
on her 97-day marriage to Max Drummey

Jordan is devastated Peter Andre has walked out of their marriage. Now she's left with only *two* massive tits.

Frankie Boyle

Stu Price: Because whatever this is, ain't working for me.
Melissa: Since when?
Stu Price: Since you f**ked that bellhop on your cruise last June. BOOM!
Alan Garner: I thought it was a bartender.

The Hangover

Money can't buy happiness . . . or put my family back together.

Elin Nordegren
(married Tiger Woods)

I was never really sober through that whole relationship.
I was out of my f**king soul.

Ashley Hamilton
on marriage to ex-Beverly Hills 90210 star Shannen Doherty

It is utter hypocrisy of this nation, which breeds illegitimate children like flies and has relegated marriage to an eccentric arrangement, to take a lofty view of Prince Charles's right to marry Camilla.

Sir Bernard Ingham

To get divorced because love has died is like selling your car because it's run out of gas.

Diane Sollee

Marriage is just the first step towards divorce.
Zsa Zsa Gabor

Peter is entitled to half of Jordan's assets. So at least he gets a Space Hopper out of it.
Frankie Boyle

The secret is removing divorce as an option. Anybody who gives themselves that option will get a divorce.
Will Smith

There is one thing I would break up over and that is if she caught me with another woman. I wouldn't stand for that.
Steve Martin

What a holler would ensue if people had to pay the minister as much to marry them as they have to pay a lawyer to get them a divorce.
Claire Trevor

Let's be honest, you know? Instead of standing there saying "'Til death do you part," let's just go, "I'll give it a shot."
Wanda Sykes

Albert Einstein, one of the greatest geniuses of all times, got divorced. They should tell you that before you get married. It shouldn't be, "Do you love her, do you want to spend the rest of your life with her?" It should be, "Do you think you're smarter than Einstein?"
Nick Griffin

It's costing $4 billion a week, the war in Iraq. That's slightly less than Paul McCartney's divorce.

David Letterman

If I was a gold-digger, I would have a lot of money in my bank account. I'd be worth millions and millions.

Heather Mills

My ex-wife once said, "He's Saddam Hussein." She said that. And I thought, "Do I hide myself in cramped underground quarters? . . . Did I execute whole villages of people and bulldoze their bodies into a pit?"

Alec Baldwin

on his acrimonious divorce with Kim Basinger

Holly Golightly: I'll never let anybody put me in a cage.
Paul: I don't want to put you in a cage. I want to love you!

Breakfast at Tiffany's

I never badmouth my ex to my kid, you should never do that, 'cos if you do, you ruin the moment when they figure it out all by themselves.

Cory Kahaney

The difference between divorce and legal separation is that legal separation gives a husband time to hide his money.

Johnny Carson

People change and forget to tell each other.

Lillian Hellman

It is amazing at how small a price may the wedding ring be placed upon a worthless hand; but, by the beauty of our law, what heaps of gold are indispensable to take it off!

Douglas Jerold

The only time my wife and I had a simultaneous orgasm was when the judge signed the divorce papers.

Woody Allen

I still love her. But she's retarded, too.

Guy Ritchie
on ex-wife Madonna

The first question was, "What was your worst break-up?" And I just kind of looked at the guy and I said, "Really? Are ya kiddin?"

Jennifer Aniston
on doing interviews for her movie *The Break-Up*

I don't know about Brad Pitt, leaving that beautiful woman to go hold orphans for Angelina. I mean, how long is that going to last?

Michael Douglas

Is it possible through hypnosis to forget someone from your recent past?

Peter Andre

I got off lightly. Think what I'd have had to pay Alyce if she had contributed anything to the relationship.

John Cleese

Now I can wear heels.
Nicole Kidman
after her divorce from Tom Cruise

It is never hard to get advice about marriage – what to wear, how much to spend, where to honeymoon – but it is frighteningly difficult to get good advice about being divorced.
Miles Kington

The cinema separated us and I will never forgive it for that.
Harrison Ford
on his divorce from first wife, Mary Marquardt

Alice: It's the only way to leave. "I don't love you anymore. Goodbye."
Dan: Supposing you do still love them?
Alice: You don't leave.
Dan: You've never left someone you still love?
Alice: Nope.
Closer

Everything looks set for Tiger Woods' wife to divorce him. Apparently she realized that once she's single she'll have a better chance of sleeping with Tiger Woods.
Conan O'Brien

Consider the number of young people all over the world
who are getting married, day in and day out, for no other
reason than that someone of the opposite sex looks well in a green
jersey or sings baritone, and then tell me that divorce hasn't reached
menacing proportions.

Robert Benchley

I guess the only way to stop divorce is to stop marriage.

Will Rogers

I just felt like I was not getting enough publicity.

Jennifer Aniston
on her divorce from Brad Pitt

Marriage is so tough, Nelson Mandela got a divorce. He got out of jail
after 27 years of torture, spent six months with his wife and said, "I
can't take this shit no more."

Chris Rock

A divorce is like an amputation; you survive it, but there's less of you

Margaret Atwood

Marriages that last are with people who do not live in Los Angeles.

Farrah Fawcett

When we got married, that was the end of the relationship,
instead of the beginning.

Allegra Mostyn-Owen
on Boris Johnson

She said, "You'll never find anyone like me again."
And I'm thinking, "I hope not!"
Does anybody end a bad relationship and say,
"By the way, do you have a twin?"
Larry Miller

In an age of social networking, speed dating and internet
chat-rooms, young people are genuinely confused about what
constitutes a relationship, let alone one that's supposed to last more
than a couple of months.
Janet Street-Porter

So trust me when I say if a guy is treating you like he doesn't give a shit
he genuinely doesn't give a shit. No exceptions.
Alex (Justin Long)
He's Just Not That Into You

Our parting is amicable and both of us still care about each other very
much but have found it increasingly difficult to maintain a normal
relationship with constant intrusion into our private lives . . .
Joint statement from
Paul McCartney and Heather Mills

She gave me an ultimatum: I had to choose between her and the ANC
. . . But when I came out of prison, I found that she had moved out and
taken the children . . . I could not give up my life in the struggle, and
she could not live with my devotion to something other than herself
and the family.
Nelson Mandela
on his first marriage to Evelyn Mase

And some sad news: the first lesbian couple to legally
get married in the state of Massachusetts has split up. They cited
irreconcilable similarities.

Jay Leno

Being divorced is like being hit by a Mack truck. If you live through it,
you start looking very carefully to the right and to the left.

Jean Kerr

You get married and hope for the best. If it doesn't work out you'll get
divorced. You can take tap with Bojangles over here.

Samantha Jones (Kim Cattrall)
Sex and The City

She is such a sad soul. It is good that it is over. Nobody was happy anyway.
I know I should preach family love and unity, but in their case . . .

Mother Teresa
on the divorce of Prince Charles and Diana

Love is grand, divorce is a hundred grand.

Anon

In California, there's a six-month waiting period for filing
for divorce, but only a 15-day waiting period for buying a handgun. It's
nice to know the government is giving us advice on how to work out
our problems.

Matt Sullivan

They say that 50 per cent of all marriages end in divorce. That's not as bad as it sounds, considering that the other 50 per cent end in death.

Anon

She's gone. She gave me a pen. I gave her my heart; she gave me a pen.

Lloyd Dobbler (John Cusack)
Say Anything

A divorce lawyer is a chameleon with a law book.

Marvin Mitchelson

A lawyer is never entirely comfortable with a friendly divorce, any more than a good mortician wants to finish his job and then have the patient sit up on the table.

Jean Kerr

Adultery – which is the only grounds for divorce in New York – is not grounds for divorce in California. As a matter of fact, adultery in Southern California is grounds for marriage.

Allan Sherman

Anybody who's been through a divorce will tell you that, at one point, they've thought murder. The line between thinking murder and doing murder isn't that major.

Oliver Stone

Conrad Hilton was very generous to me in the divorce settlement. He gave me 5,000 Gideon Bibles.

Zsa Zsa Gabor

Divorce is the one human tragedy that reduces everything to cash.
Rita Mae Brown

I hardly said a word to my wife until I said "yes" to divorce.
John Milius

I swear, if you existed, I'd divorce you.
Martha
Who's Afraid of Virginia Woolf?

Only time can heal your broken heart, just as only time can heal his
broken arms and legs.
Miss Piggy

They say that breaking up is hard to do – but it's much easier with a
restraining order and a Rottweiler.
Dakota Shepard

A relationship, I think, is like a shark. You know?
It has to constantly move forward or it dies. And I think what we got
on our hands is a dead shark.
Alvy Singer (Woody Allen)
Annie Hall

Marriage is really tough because
you have to deal with feelings and lawyers.
Richard Pryor

Husband: Pack up your things. I just won the lottery!
Wife: Shall I pack for warm weather or cold?
Husband: I don't care. Just so long as you're out of the house by noon.

I'd like to give divorce a good name.
Geraldo Rivera

In every marriage more than a week old, there are grounds for divorce.
The trick is to find, and continue to find, grounds for marriage.
Robert Anderson

In Hollywood, after you get a little success,
the next thing you usually get is a divorce.
Dan Dailey

Oliver Rose: I worked my ass off for you and the kids to have a nice life
and you owe me a reason that makes sense. I want to hear it.
Barbara Rose: Because. When I watch you eat, when I see you asleep . . .
When I look at you lately, I just want to smash your face in.
The War of the Roses

In Hollywood, an equitable divorce settlement means each party
getting 50 percent of the publicity.
Lauren Bacall

In Palm Springs, they think homelessness is caused
by bad divorce lawyers.
G. B. Trudeau

My divorce came as a complete surprise to me. That's what happens when you haven't been home in 18 years.

Lee Trevino

My mother always said, "Don't marry for money, divorce for money."

Wendy Liebman

Staying married may have long-term benefits. You can elicit much more sympathy from friends over a bad marriage than you ever can from a good divorce.

P. J. O'Rourke

When two people decide to get a divorce, it isn't a sign that they "don't understand" one another, but a sign that they have, at last, begun to.

Helen Rowland

Staying Single

It's a funny thing that when a man hasn't anything on earth to worry about, he goes off and gets married.
Robert Frost

I respect a woman too much to marry her.
Sylvester Stallone

A man in love is incomplete until he is married. Then he's finished.
Zsa Zsa Gabor

I, marry? Oh, I could never bring myself to do it. I would have been in mortal misery all my life for fear my wife might say, "That's a pretty little thing," after I had finished a picture.
Edgar Degas

I think I'd rather get run over by a train.
Madonna
on getting married again

Jane's Aunt: It must be so hard to watch your younger sister
get married before you.

Jane: Yes. Then I remember that I still get to have hot hate sex with
random strangers and I feel so much better!

27 Dresses

I'm anal retentive. I'm a workaholic. I have insomnia. And I'm a
control freak. That's why I'm not married. Who could stand me?

Madonna

If men knew how women pass the time when they are alone,
they'd never marry.

O Henry

Any intelligent woman who reads the marriage contract, and then goes
into it, deserves all the consequences.

Isadora Duncan

You young guys are looking up here going, "I'm never going to get
married." That's what I thought, but how many times can you go home,
watch SportsCenter, order a pizza and jerk off before that gets boring?
I'll tell you how many times: 11, 556.

Nick DiPaolo

Women now have choices. They can be married, not married, have a
job, not have a job, be married with children, unmarried with children.
Men have the same choice we've always had: work or prison.

Tim Allen

Instead of getting married again, I'm going to find a woman I don't like and just give her a house.

Rod Stewart

I belong to Bridegrooms Anonymous. Whenever I feel like getting married, they send over a lady in a housecoat and hair curlers to burn my toast for me.

Dick Martin

When did being alone become the modern-day equivalent of being a leper? Will Manhattan restaurants soon be divided up into sections – smoking/non-smoking, single/non-single?

Carrie Bradshaw (Sarah Jessica Parker)
Sex and The City

I'm scared of commitment . . . it's for that reason I'm into kinky sex. It doesn't get me off, it's just a lot harder to fall in love when someone's dressed as a baby and pissing on you.

Ben Davis

I had no one to hold. What if this was my life: attending weddings, sitting in pews, listening to 'I do's, perpetually wishing for someone to share my life with? Where the f**k was the alcohol?

Stephanie Klein
Straight up and Dirty

I thought when I was 41, I would be married with kids. Well, to be
honest, I thought I'd be divorced with weekend access.
Sean Hughes

I've never been married, but I tell people I'm divorced so they won't
think something's wrong with me.
Elayne Boosler

I've sometimes thought of marrying, and then I've thought again.
Noel Coward

I think marriage is a marvellous thing for other people,
like going to the stake.
Philip Larkin

If I ever marry, it will be on a sudden impulse – as a man shoots himself.
H.L. Mencken

Sometimes I wonder if men and women really suit each other. Perhaps
they should live next door and just visit now and then.
Katherine Hepburn

Love is blind and marriage is the institution for the blind.
James Graham

I have come to the conclusion never again to think of marrying, and for this reason, I can never be satisfied with anyone who would be blockhead enough to have me.
Abraham Lincoln

Bachelors know more about women than married men; if they didn't, they'd be married too.
H. L. Mencken

The only good husbands stay bachelors:
they're too considerate to get married.
Finley Peter Dunne

I'd marry again if I found a man who had 15 million and would sign over half of it to me before the marriage and guarantee he'd be dead within a year.
Bette Davis

Some of us are becoming the men we wanted to marry.
Gloria Steinem

We're not actually married. We've been together a long time. 'Girlfriend' doesn't seem significant enough a term to describe the relationship; 'lodger' – she hates that.
Sean Lock

I can't believe Vanessa, my bride, my one true love, the woman who taught me the beauty of monogamy, was a fembot . . . all along. Wait a tick. That means I'm single again! Oh, behave! Yeah!

Austin Powers (Mike Myers)
The Spy Who Shagged Me

It would have been a wonderful wedding – had it not been mine.

Erma Bombeck

Any young man who is unmarried at the age of 21 is a menace to the community.

Brigham Young

Oh, I don't mind going to weddings, just as long as it's not my own.

Tom Waits

I never married because I have three pets at home that answer the same purpose as a husband. I have a dog that growls every morning, a parrot that swears all afternoon and a cat that comes home late at night.

Marie Corelli

Monica: Chandler and I have this pact not to have sex until the wedding.
Ross: A no-sex pact, huh? I seem to have one of those going with every woman in America.

Friends

I don't believe in marriage, certainly not in this business. The truth is that you get married and in a year or two they clean you out.

Simon Cowell

My ex-girlfriend called. She's getting married; she called to tell me. Yeah, she called. She wanted closure. I said, "What part of us not talking the last year seemed open to you?"

Cash Levy

I'm missing the bride gene. I should be put in a test tube and studied.

Carrie Bradshaw (Sarah Jessica Parker)
Sex and The City

My boyfriend likes role-play. He likes to pretend we're married. He waits until I go to bed, then he looks at porn and has a wank.

Joanna Neary

Marrying Again

I kind of wanted to get married to get my first marriage out of the way.
John Heffron

I've only slept with men I've been married to.
How many women can make that claim?
Elizabeth Taylor

I have been married five times. I'm a perfectionist, so I kept trying until
I got it right, which I have, I'm happy to report. Suzy Amis is a keeper.
James Cameron

Wow. This is the first time I've walked down the aisle without the
possibility of it ending in divorce.
Ross (David Schwimmer)
at Chandler and Monica's wedding, *Friends*

She had been married so often she bought a drip-dry wedding dress.
Chic Murray

I'm an excellent housekeeper.
Every time I get a divorce, I keep the house.
Zsa Zsa Gabor

I'm going through a divorce now. This is the second one
and, like baseball, I'm not gonna get three strikes. I've been living by
myself for five years and I'm very comfortable. I can play my guitar
when I want to.
Buddy Guy

I am thinking of taking a fifth wife. Why not? Solomon had a thousand
wives and he is a synonym for wisdom.
John Barrymore

I'm the only man who has a marriage license made out,
"To Whom It May Concern".
Mickey Rooney

I think that everyone should get married at least once, so you can see
what a silly, outdated institution it is.

Twice-divorced
Madonna

Marriage is a lot like the army: everyone complains, but you'd be
surprised at the large number that re-enlist.
James Garner

I'm a very committed wife. And I should be committed too – for being
married so many times.
Elizabeth Taylor

My toughest fight was with my first wife.
Muhammad Ali

She's been married so many times she has rice marks on her face.
Henny Youngman

The sad truth, Janine had to admit as she drove over to the Empire Grill, was that she'd gone and divorced a man she could talk to and married one she couldn't.
Richard Russo
Empire Falls

For her fifth wedding, the bride wore black
and carried a scotch and soda.
Phyllis Battelle

I always say a girl must get married for love – and just keep on getting married until she finds it.
Zsa Zsa Gabor

I've been married three times –
and each time I married the right person.
Margaret Mead

When a divorced man marries a divorced woman, four get into bed.
The Talmud

When widows exclaim loudly against second marriages, I would always lay a wager that the man, if not the wedding day, is absolutely fixed on.
Henry Fielding

A lot of people have asked me how short I am. Since my last divorce, I
think I'm about $100,000 short.
Mickey Rooney

I married a few people I shouldn't have, but haven't we all?
Mamie Van Doren

Marriage is like wine. It is not properly judged until the second glass.
Douglas William Jerrold

Round up all the divorced men and keep them in a pound. That way,
you get their whole history before you take one home.
Samantha Jones (Kim Cattrall)
Sex and The City

I never hated a man enough to give him his diamonds back.
Zsa Zsa Gabor

I believe in the institution of marriage
and I intend to keep trying until I get it right.
Richard Pryor

Forsaking All Others

The grass looks greener . . . but it's Astroturf.
Anon

All husbands are alike, but they have different faces
so you can tell them apart.
Ogden Nash

If I didn't have you, someone else would do.
Tim Minchin

Why buy a book when you can join the library?
Lily Savage (Paul O'Grady)

You just can't maraud through life f**king whoever you'd like . . .
which is a shame because I wish I could actually do that.
That's the compromise.
Russell Brand

One of the first things a bridegroom learns is that a man can't fool his wife as easily as his mother.

Anon

Grandad: This brings back so many memories of my wedding day.
Crowded church, everyone in their finery,
and Jane, oh, Jane was so beautiful, breathtaking she was.
Sue: Dad, mum's name was Joan.
Grandad: I know. She had this gorgeous friend called Jane.
Real stunner.

Outnumbered

My wife uses fabric softener. I never knew what that stuff was for. Then I noticed women coming up to me, sniffing, then saying under their breath, "Married!" and walking away. Fabric softeners are how our wives mark their territory. We can take off the ring, but it's hard to get that April-fresh scent out of your clothes.

Andy Rooney

On rare occasions one does hear of a miraculous case of a married couple falling in love after marriage, but on close examination it will be found that it is a mere adjustment to the inevitable.

Emma Goldman

It's really hard to maintain a one-on-one relationship if the other person is not going to allow me to be with other people.

Axl Rose

If you marry a man who cheats on his wife, you'll be married to a man
who cheats on his wife.
Ann Landers

Let me get this straight, honey. I can't sleep with anybody else ever
again for the rest of my life, and if this doesn't work out, you get to
keep all my stuff?
Bobby Slayton

Michael Jordan is the only athlete you can sleep with and I wouldn't get
mad, as long as you got something signed. You gotta bring back a ball, a
hat or something. You can't just give away that shit for free.
Aries Spears

I suffer from short-term memory loss. I'll give you an example: on my
honeymoon, I took my wedding ring off to go swimming in the sea . . .
and I had sex with someone.
Adam Bloom

Women who marry early are often overly enamoured of the kind
of man who looks great in wedding pictures and passes the maid of
honour his telephone number.
Anna Quindlen

Bigamy is one way of avoiding the painful publicity of divorce and the expense of alimony.
Oliver Herford

My marriage ended on my wedding day.
Bianca Jagger

"What's a couple?" I asked my mum. She said, "Two or three". Which probably explains why her marriage collapsed.
Josie Long

In a survey, six percent said a good place to have sex is a wedding reception. I remember when you just kissed the bride.
Jay Leno

An open marriage is nature's way of telling you that you need a divorce.
Ann Landers

When a girl marries she exchanges the attentions of many men for the inattention of one.
Helen Rowland

Newt [Gingrich] is so pro-marriage, he can't stop doing it. He is so morally upright that he's only had sex after he was married. Just not always to the woman he was married to.

Jimmy Kimmel

Marriage means commitment. Of course, so does insanity.

Anon

Never get a tattoo with someone's name on it unless you're ready to get another one put over it.

Billy Bob Thornton

The trouble with wedlock is that there's not enough wed and too much lock.

Christopher Morley

Men look at women the way men look at cars. Everyone looks at Ferraris. Now and then we like a pickup truck, and we all buy station wagons.

Tim Allen

Marriage is for ever. It's like cement.

Peter O'Toole

I promise to love, honour and cherish you –
for about two days a month.
Bill Dwyer
on polygamist wedding vows

Bigamy is having one wife too many. Monogamy is the same.
Oscar Wilde

Marriage is based on the theory that when a man discovers a particular
brand of beer exactly to his taste, he should at once throw in his job
and go to work in the brewery.
George Nathan

If the grass looks greener on the other side of the fence, it's because they
take better care of it.
Cecil Selig

Happily Ever After

I often wonder when the wedding couple will realize just how much
hard work they've taken on by consecrating that quirky emotion called
love into the formal tie of marriage.

Lois Smith Brady

Marriage isn't supposed to make you happy –
it's supposed to make you married.

Frank Pittman

If the marriage ain't happy, ain't nobody happy.

Scott Gardner

The first part of our marriage was very happy. Then, on the way back
from the ceremony . . .

Henny Youngman

Weeping bride, laughing wife; laughing bride, weeping wife.

German proverb

All marriages are mixed marriages.
Chantal Saperstein

Remember, the most adorable bride of today will be someone's mother-in-law in the future.
Anon

The most important marriage skill is listening to your partner in a way that they can't possibly doubt that you love them.
Diane Sollee

Eighteen is too young to get married. You can't even buy alcohol. If you can't drink, how are you going to make your marriage work?
Lisa Landry

Marriage is give and take. You'd better give it to her
or she'll take it anyway.
Anon

Well, the old theory was "Marry an older man because
they're more mature". But the new theory is "Men don't mature –
marry a young one".
Rita Rudner

Katy [Perry] is sexy, which is good because if I don't have an orgasm every 15 or 16 minutes, I can become very difficult. But, if she's going to marry me, she's going to bloody learn how to cook.
Russell Brand

When you marry your mistress you create a job vacancy.
James Goldsmith

What you don't catch a glimpse of on your wedding day – because how could you? – is that some days you will hate your spouse, that you will look at him and regret ever exchanging a word with him, let alone a ring and bodily fluids.
Nick Hornby

Never marry a man who hates his mother
because he'll end up hating you.
Jill Bennett

My idea of heaven is a great big baked potato
and someone to share it with.
Oprah Winfrey

The surest way to be alone is to get married.
Gloria Steinem

If you are going to argue, argue naked.
Anon

I'm convinced marriage isn't a natural state, but if you're persistent you learn to love the companionship and then you learn to love your companion.
Dan Harper

They dream in courtship, but in wedlock wake.
Alexander Pope

Being married is like having a colour television set. You never want to go back to black and white.

Danny Perosa

Men have a much better time of it than women. For one thing, they marry later; for another thing, they die earlier.

H. L. Mencken

Keep on holding hands because if you let go you'll split each other.

Wedding guest

Gay Byrne's

advice to Tommy Tiernan and Yvonne McMahon

Ruth and I are happily incompatible.

Billy Graham

The best romance is inside marriage; the finest love stories come after the wedding, not before.

Irving Stone

I still fancy Meera [Syal] in her granny suit. At least I know what the future holds. Everyone in a relationship should dress up to be very, very old. It would help them work out how they will feel about each other in the future.

Sanjeev Bhaskar

Two imperfect people got married and it was the promise that made the marriage. And when our children were growing up, it wasn't a house that protected them; and it wasn't our love that protected them – it was that promise.

Thornton Wilder
The Skin of Our Teeth

I should have suspected my husband was lazy. On our wedding day, his mother told me: "I'm not losing a son; I'm gaining a couch".

Phyllis Diller

I'll choose a marriage over a wedding any day.

Sue Townshend

Getting married is insanity; I mean it's a risk – who knows if you're going to be together forever? But you both say "we're going to take this chance, in the same spirit".

Cate Blanchett

After I got that marriage license I went across from the license bureau to a bar for a drink. The bartender said, "What will you have, sir?" and I said, "A glass of hemlock."

Ernest Hemingway

One advantage of marriage is that when you fall out of love with each other, it keeps you together until maybe you fall in love again.

Judith Viorst

Why do married men gain weight while bachelors don't? Bachelors go to the refrigerator, see nothing they want, then go to bed. Married guys go to the bed, see nothing they want, then go to the refrigerator.

Anon

Bride's father hands a note to the groom: "GOODS DELIVERED ARE NOT RETURNABLE."
Groom gives a note back to the father: "CONTRACT VOID IF SEAL IS BROKEN."

Anon

They're thinking about letting priests get married now – well, not to each other. The Pope said it's a bad idea. He said it would weaken their faith because, after about four years of being married, most people start to think, "Oh, there is no God."

Mark Brazill

Marriage is a lottery, but you can't tear up your ticket if you lose.

F. M. Knowles

Look, I'll tell you about the age thing – if he dies, he dies!

Joan Collins

Marry a woman from the mountain and you'll marry the mountain.

Irish Proverb

Before marriage, a man will go home and lie awake all night thinking about something you said; after marriage, he'll go to sleep before you finish saying it.

Helen Rowland

Once a boy becomes a man, he's a man all his life, but a woman is only sexy until she becomes your wife.

Al Bundy

My wife tells me that if I ever decide to leave, she's coming with me.

Jon Bon Jovi

Marriage is like a besieged castle; those who are on the outside wish to get in; and those who are on the inside wish to get out.

Arabic Proverb

To marry unequally is to suffer equally.

Henri Frederic Amiel

Martha Phelps (Margaret Dumont): I'm afraid that after we've been married a while a beautiful girl will come along, and you'll forget all about me.
Wolf J. Flywheel (Groucho Marx): Don't be silly. I'll write you twice a week.

The Big Store

For a marriage to have any chance, every day at least six things should go unsaid.

Anon

What counts in making a happy marriage is not so much how
compatible you are, but how you deal with incompatibility.
Leo Tolstoy

If variety is the spice of life, marriage is the big can of leftover Spam.
Johnny Carson

Wedding: the point at which a man stops toasting a woman
and begins roasting her.
Helen Rowland

I've been married now for fifteen years, on and off.
John Bishop

Beat your wife on the wedding day, and your married life will be happy.
Japanese Proverb

The difficulty with marriage is that we fall in love with a personality,
but must live with a character.
Peter De Vries

Why can't women tell jokes? Because we marry them!
Kathy Lette

Delighted and frankly amazed that Diana is prepared to take me on.
Prince Charles

Spouse: someone who'll stand by you through all the trouble you
wouldn't have had if you'd stayed single.
Anon

I have yet to hear a man ask for advice on
how to combine marriage and a career.
Gloria Steinem

The problem with marriage is that it ends every night after making love,
and it must be rebuilt every morning before breakfast.
Gabriel García Márquez

After the chills and fever of love, how nice is the 98.6° of marriage!
Mignon McLaughlin

The bonds of matrimony are like any other bonds – they mature slowly.
Peter De Vries

It was strange to see what delight we married people have to see these
poor fools decoyed into our condition, every man and wife gazing and
smiling at them.
Samuel Pepys

Bride: A woman with a fine prospect of happiness behind her.
Ambrose Bierce

You marry someone, you make babies with that person and the more
babies that she has the more it erodes the parts of her body that makes
you want to have sex with her. That's the real reason that married
couples don't go out. You don't want to sit your wife on a bar stool and
then watch it slowly disappear.
Frankie Boyle

An old man who marries a young wife grows younger –
but she grows older.
Folk Proverb

All marriages are happy.
It's the living together afterward that causes all the trouble.
Raymond Hull

The funny thing is that although we place so much energy and
importance on our wedding day, it isn't the biggest day of our life. The
biggest day of your life is every day thereafter.
Laura Wolf

Mrs. Vice turned to the weddings page. She liked to look at the smiling
brides and imagine how miserable they would soon be.
Kelly Easton
The Outlandish Adventures of Liberty Aimes

Do you know what it means to come home at night to a woman who'll
give you a little love, a little affection, a little tenderness? It means
you're in the wrong house, that's what it means.
Henny Youngman

I'm happily married. Unfortunately my husband's not, but you can't
have everything.
Jo Brand

Swans mate for life, and look how bad-tempered they are.
Jeff Green

I have a theory that the secret of marital happiness is simple: drink in
different pubs to your other half.
Jilly Cooper

In my experience, the married man's allowance is . . .
about once a month.
Hugh Dennis

Wedlock is the deep, deep peace of the double bed
after the hurly-burly of the chaise lounge.
Mrs Patrick Campbell

A sweetheart is a bottle of wine, a wife is a wine bottle.
Baudelaire

Love matches are made by people who are content, for a month of
honey, to condemn themselves to a life of vinegar.
Countess of Blessington

The sense of romance and adventure that you feel as you take
your wedding wows on that bright Saturday afternoon in June
inevitably gives way to familiarity and even boredom, often as early as
8:30 that evening.
Dave Barry

I was thinking about Henry VIII the other day. Do you think he ever thought, "F**k, maybe it's me?"
Russell Howard

Before marriage, a man declares that he would lay down his life to serve you; after marriage, he won't even lay down his newspaper to talk to you.
Helen Rowland

When you've been married for a while it gets a bit boring in bed. The other day I said to my husband: "I can't remember the last time we had sex." He yelled back: "We're having it now!"
Jo Brand

Twenty years of romance make a woman look like a ruin; but 20 years of marriage make her something like a public building.
Oscar Wilde

There is more to marriage than four bare legs in a bed.
John Heywood

For marriage to be a success, every woman and every man should have her and his own bathroom. The end.
Catherine Zeta Jones

I think it should be like dog licences. I think you should have to renew marriage licences every five years.
John Cleese

One cardinal rule of marriage should never be forgotten: GIVE
LITTLE, GIVE SELDOM, AND ABOVE ALL, GIVE
GRUDGINGLY. Otherwise what could have been a proper marriage
could become an orgy of sexual lust.

Ruth Smythers
Instruction and Advice for the Young Bride, 1894

Marriage is like the Witness Protection Program:
you get new clothes, you live in the suburbs and you're not allowed to
see your friends anymore.

Jeremy Hardy

— Do you think marriage is a lottery?
— No. With a lottery you do have a slight chance.

The Two Ronnies

In a happy marriage it is the wife who provides the climate, the husband
the landscape.

Gerald Brenan

My mother-in-law broke up my marriage. My wife came home from
work one day and found me in bed with her.

Lenny Bruce

Marrying a man is like buying something you've been admiring for a
long time in a shop window. You may love it when you get home, but it
doesn't always go with everything else in the house.

Jean Kerr

Inertia accounts for two-thirds of marriages.
But love accounts for the other third.
Woody Allen

The woman cries before the wedding; the man afterward.
Anon

I was married by a judge. I should have asked for a jury.
Groucho Marx

The wise bride will permit a maximum of two brief sexual experiences
weekly during the first months of marriage. As time goes by she should
make every effort to reduce this frequency.
Ruth Smythers
Instruction and Advice for the Young Bride, 1894

Marriage has no guarantees. If that's what you're looking for, go live
with a car battery.
Erma Bombeck

Marriage is very exciting for about two weeks, then you find your
spouse starts to do little things that irritate you a bit.
One of the little irritating things my husband does is waking up. I
do little things that annoy him too, like snoring. That annoys him.
Especially when we're having sex.
Jo Brand

The gift of real love is having someone who'll go the distance with you. Someone who, when the wedding day limo breaks down, is willing to share a seat on the bus.

Oprah Winfrey

I came from a big family. As a matter of fact, I never got to sleep alone until I was married.

Lewis Grizzard

A married couple celebrating their golden wedding anniversary decided to give each other gifts in the form of epitaphs. The man wrote, "Here's my one and only wife, cold as ever." The woman wrote, "Here's my one and only husband, stiff at last."

Anon

There's only one way to have a happy marriage, and as soon as I learn what it is I'll get married again.

Clint Eastwood

This is the fairy-tale romance of the century. Girl meets boy. Girl loses boy. Boy marries another girl. Girl becomes boy's mistress. Other girl dies tragically. And they all live happily ever after.

Stephen Colbert

on Prince Charles and Camilla Parker-Bowles

Women, once you get married he will never lick your pussy again . . . for ever, ever . . . Don't get me wrong, he'll give it one coat, but he ain't gonna put the finish on it like he used to.

Chris Rock

We were happily married for eight months. Unfortunately, we were married for four and a half years.

Nick Faldo

You can be married and bored or single and lonely. There ain't no happiness nowhere. That's right. Marriage is some boring-ass shit.

Chris Rock

A good wife should expect to have reduced sexual contacts to once a week by the end of the first year of marriage and to once a month by the end of the fifth year of marriage.

Ruth Smythers
Instruction and Advice for the Young Bride, 1894

I read that the secret to a happy marriage is for a man to marry a woman who's far more attractive than him. This is according to the results of a scientific investigation carried out by a really ugly scientist.

Frankie Boyle

Brides aren't happy – they are just triumphant.

John Barrymore

By all means marry; if you get a good wife, you'll be happy. If you get a bad one, you'll become a philosopher.

Socrates

There is no happy ever after. Weddings are an out-of-date ritual that offer nothing concrete to the modern, independent women but are still sold as an answer to every dissatisfaction she might have with her life.

Phillip Hodson

a fellow of the British Association for Counselling and Psychotherapy,
on post-nuptial depression (PND)

You win or the relationship wins.

Terry Hargrave

Marriage is a lottery in which men stake their liberty
and women their happiness.

Anon

A sound marriage is not based on complete frankness;
it is based on a sensible reticence.

Morris L Ernst

I look forward to the several months of happiness Alex and I have
ahead, and I feel certain that he'll be one of the most wonderful, loving
husbands I ever have.

Katie Price (Michael Deacon)

I think people really marry far too much; it is such a lottery, after all,
and for a poor woman a very doubtful happiness.

Queen Victoria

Samantha: You know marriage doesn't guarantee a happy ending, just an ending.
Samantha Jones (Kim Cattrall)
Sex and The City

It is not your love that sustains the marriage but, from now on, the marriage that sustains your love.
Dietrich Bonhoeffer

Mom and Pop were just a couple of kids when they got married. He was 18, she was 16, and I was three.
Billie Holiday

Married women don't have pussies; married women have vaginas. If you go to a wedding and the woman's throwing the bouquet, she's not throwing the bouquet, she's throwing the pussy: "I won't be needing this no more."
Chris Rock

Mutual love, a little hatred and staying the hell away from each other.
Denis Leary

If you want to read about love and marriage, you've got to buy two separate books.
Alan King

Some of the most important words in marriage are "Maybe you are right" and "Let's try it your way." As a good friend of mine said to me after his first year of marriage: "I finally learned that the sun will come up tomorrow if we try it her way".

Jeff Herring

My parents stayed together for their entire married lives and they didn't regret a single day of it until their murder-suicide.

Frankie Boyle

Floyd's moving on, I'm moving on too; I'm just doing it in my own order. I'm gonna get the wedding dress, and then I'm gonna have a baby, and then I'm gonna die, and then I'm gonna meet a super-cute guy in heaven.

Liz Lemon (Tina Fey)

30 Rock

Love doesn't exist, that's what I'm trying to tell you guys. And I'm not picking on love, 'cos I don't think friendship exists either

John Beckwith (Owen Wilson)

expounding to a group of children
at a wedding, *The Wedding Crashers*

Jordan says that, during the five years she's been married, she's only gone out 20 times. It's just a pity she only came home five times.

Frankie Boyle

If you are afraid of loneliness, don't marry.
Anton Pavlovich Chekhov

Make love as often as you can and pay off your credit card debt every month. Put up a little sign somewhere where you will both see it every day that says, "Make love, not debt".
Bill Doherty

The trouble is you almost have to marry a man before you can find out the sort of wife he needs; and usually it's exactly the sort you are not.
Willa Cather

The secret of a good marriage is forgiving your partner for marrying you in the first place.
Sacha Guitry

Try praising your wife, even if it does frighten her at first.
Billy Sunday

Adam and Eve had an ideal marriage. He didn't have to hear about all the men she could have married, and she didn't have to hear about the way his mother cooked.
Kimberley Broyles

The very fact that we make such a to-do over golden weddings indicates our amazement at human endurance. The celebration is more in the nature of a reward for stamina.
Ilka Chase

More marriages might survive if the partners realized that sometimes the better comes after the worse.
Doug Larson

Bruce [Jenner] and my mom have been married for 20 years – I'm going to get to 50! He's kind of handsome. I kind of love him.
Khloe Kardashian
on her whirlwind marriage to Lamar Odom

Having someone wonder where you are when you don't come home at night is a very old human need.
Margaret Mead

Marriage is for women the commonest mode of livelihood, and the total amount of undesired sex endured by women is probably greater in marriage than in prostitution.
Bertrand Russell

How would I make a marriage work?
Tell my wife that she looks pretty even if she looks like a truck.
Ricky
age 10

When I eventually met Mr Right
I had no idea that his first name was Always.
Rita Rudner

You can't buy love, but you can pay heavily for it.
Henny Youngman

Our wedding was many years ago.
The celebration continues to this day.
Gene Perret

A wedding anniversary is the celebration of love, trust, partnership,
tolerance and tenacity. The order varies for any given year.
Paul Sweeney

When it's right you can't say
Who is kissing whom.
Gregory Orr

The man who says his wife can't take a joke forgets that she took him.
Oscar Wilde

A little boy asked his father, "Daddy, how much does it cost to get
married?" The father replied, "I don't know son, I'm still paying."
Anon

All those 'and they lived happily ever after' fairy-tale endings
need to be changed to "... and they began the very hard work of
making their marriages happy."
Linda Miles